JESUS IS
THE STREET

Omar Gaitán

ADULAM EDITIONS

Gaitán, Arturo Omar
Jesus is the street. - 1a ed. - Rafael Castillo : Adulam, 2013.
144 p. ; 20x14 cm.

Traducido por: Swindoll Orville
ISBN 978-987-29085-0-8

1. Vida Cristiana. I. Orville, Swindoll, trad. II. Título
CDD 248.5

Fecha de catalogación:30/01/2013

ISBN 978-987-29085-0-8

Design: Oscar Vena – oscarvena@gmail.com

Contributors: Belén Rodriguez, Graciela Buffon, Vanesa Stratta.

Protected under law 11.723

Gratitude

To my friends from the streets

To those who have helped me

To my first pastors

To the memory of my parents

To my wife

To my children

To my pastor and friend

To my fellow soldiers in the fight

To those who have made this book possible

I can't name many others that I would like to. It would be impossible for me. But I recall them every day, living the way they taught me to or remembering them in some anecdote.

Prologue

O mar Gaitán is unique! After listening to his stories —or after reading them— you begin to feel like he is the personification of a saying I heard years ago: We've been doing so much with so little for so long, that we have come to believe that we can do anything with almost nothing. Omar is an inspiration to my faith in God. He thinks creatively; he acts boldly; he waits patiently.

Years ago I began to understand that no one learns to live by faith without facing many obstacles and enduring many troubles. Omar has suffered much, but he seems to have never lost faith in a God who does wonders. After reading the accounts in this little book, you too will see how God uses simple people and simple situations in amazing ways.

When Omar asked me to translate his book from Spanish into English, I had little idea of the effect it would have on me personally. My wife and I have read with fascination his captivating accounts of lives that have been transformed, nightmares that have been turned into joyful dreams, impossible hurdles that have been overcome. I have compared him to Philip in the book of Acts, a true apostle to the despised and disenfranchised, always expecting to see God doing something wonderful that reveals his love and power.

I think you will be glad this book reached your hands. Let its stories awaken your faith, your compassion, and your desire to serve God with total dedication.

Orville Swindoll

Preface

$\mathcal{A}$ nyone acquainted with Omar Gaitán knows that his life is an example of service. In the pages of this book you will find anecdotes, accounts, and real life experiences that will make you laugh, cry, reflect and meditate.

Omar relates his testimony with many interesting details. His childhood in Indio Rico, his conversion there, the move to Buenos Aires seeking to prepare himself to serve God, and his marriage to Carmen, faithful companion in his life and work. He tells of his missionary activity, his children (including the tragic experience of the loss of Sarah, his oldest, to her heavenly home), his beginnings in La Matanza, where he learned and put into practice simple counsel and principles that changed his life and ministry. And he tells of the beginning of the farms, with Adulam in Virrey del Pino and other places that were added through the years. I am sure that as this book reaches your hands, another farm will be appearing somewhere through Omar's faith, prayer and vision.

As his pastor I meet with him from time to time. Every encounter is full of surprises. He always has more than one advance project and service in his hands. And he consults with me with great respect. I always wind up backing his faith.

I have the conviction that after reading this book you will want to learn more about the work that Omar is directing. You will discover much more than what he tells here. Dozens of young people rescued from a wayward life will tell you with much gratitude what this man and his wife have meant to them.

You will understand through those farms how to be rich while having few material goods. Every person is a testimony of the work of the author of this book. I recommend its reading to you, knowing that it will be a valuable contribution to your devotion and service for the Lord.

Hugo Baravalle

Table of contents

Prologue
to the second edition

To God be the glory! He has made possible what seemed unthinkable: Here we present the second edition of "YO SOY LA CALLE". With the distribution of the first edition we have seen an abundant harvest: Amazing occurrences that have made possible the extension of God's kingdom. Exciting and useful encounters. Testimonies of God's great power. Doubts that have been clarified and responsibilities assumed by many believers in different places. New works were also initiated, homes, work among addicts, work with children and others. Some came to know Christ through the book. Many decided to help us as they became aware of the work through the book. And we could mention dozens of other facts, besides the ones that we don't yet know, or have forgotten. God was very good to us, as we believe he will be as we initiate this new edition.

We're still working, faithful in the gap where the Lord placed us. Never without difficulties, but with the same enthusiasm and love. We continue without growing weary of doing good to others. By his grace we can still tell of his wonders and miracles that encourage us to continue along the pathway to heaven; that help us to grow in the knowledge of God and to increase the faith of many.

We're going for more! More of God, new readers, new friends, new information, new properties, new brothers and sisters, more testimonies that will provide the obvious evidence that God is with us.

As always, we are at your disposition, for whatever we can do for you.

We expect to see you soon...

Omar Gaitán

Our humble story

Introduction

What follows is a simple story about simple people; a story that reveals again God's great love for people. John 3:16 shows us that God gave up his Son for us simply because he loved us. I believe that for any father, it is easier to surrender himself rather than his son; that's the way God showed us how much he loved us: he gave us Jesus.

The following account is a little summary of a great testimony; a small sample of what God is able to do with people that at the outset don't even know what to request when they pray, but they place themselves in God's hands. He did everything else. Although from the beginning I was willing to place all my life and all that I had at his disposition, I knew that "my treasure" was not something of interest to anyone else.

Long ago a pastor told me that the things of God were free, but that it would take my entire life to learn how much they really cost. I have discovered that is true; for there is nothing worth more than what God has done for us. We owe everything to him. That is the reason it has been so costly to give and to give ourselves so that others might have at least a word and a piece of bread. We had to respond in some way to the great love we had received!

For many of us the fact that we are really poor has been our life style; it wasn't simply a question of existing, and nothing more.

We had to live, we wanted to do it, and since we didn't have everything we needed, we had to get by with what we could get and be satisfied with that. I began to live that way by inheritance or accident, and then I adopted the style as my own; and I assumed it would never be different. Of course when you want to live, and you know God, and receive his abundant blessing, you become very grateful, and this results in a real, though strange, prosperity: real, because no one can deny that we have made great progress in every way; and strange, because now that we have prospered, we continue to be dependent and in need of God, as if nothing had changed.

This is the genuine life of many that come from the street. Not everyone who lives there is miserable, nor are they all individuals that, discontent with what they have, try to get more by illegal means. On the street you learn everything: the bad and the good. It is well known that the street teaches bad habits; but it is also true that the sidewalks are full of poor people who are very generous in sharing what they have, and congenial old folks that are wise teachers without classroom or salary. God doesn't lose time, and if he seeks among the poor for those who will later be his children, there must be a reason.

Allow me to invite you to read this account of lives placed in God's hands; of tears that have born new believers and of garbage transformed into homes, furniture, food and eternal life.

1.

Jesus goes to villages

esus is good. He likes villages. He even goes to those that don't appear on the maps. And of course, he reaches out to those with strange names. He went to my village of Indio Rico and found me there, in a web of misery. He gave me his wonderful message of love and he saved me for all eternity. I can never repay him for such generosity!

After that encounter I was never again the same, for since that day I have always had someone to guide me along the right path, and I still try to follow him with joy and faith, in spite of the difficulties that we all know are never lacking when we seek to be faithful to our Christian calling.

In villages like mine are often found the most unlikely romantic incidents, from which tales are spun that later appear in books and novels. Meeting Jesus was like living one of those love stories told by the older residents of the town. Even today, as I write, my heart is still filled with the same emotion that I felt then.

Jesus, in his genius, delivered my family from the plague of alcohol; he even did it for those of us who never were addicted. Alcohol turns homes into an ugly place. And it is difficult to grow up there, since almost always such a problem is surrounded by an endless number of problems as evil as itself —sometimes worse— such as misery, pain, abandonment, violence, fear and the likes. When anyone is given to drink in a home, it is almost as bad as if all were drinking. Often, such habits provoke children to flee from their home even at an early age, or at least to be at home as little as possible during the day. Perhaps that is due to their search for happiness, or maybe because their survival instinct leads them to seek a different kind of life. And when a person is poor he has few alternatives from which to choose. Almost always, after trying one option after another, he winds up in the street, and the street... well, it's the street! You already know that most of the time nothing good turns up there. Even that may not be entirely the case, since Jesus also went into the streets to seek those he loved... and that's where he found me.

Who could have ever imagined that? Right there, in the place about which we all made fun, was the solution that I had worn myself out seeking in so many other places. In the evangelical church on the other side of the railroad track! It was the poorest place in the village; nobody ever dreamed of finding anything good over there. Maybe it was God himself that allowed something good to be found there, surrounded by mystery and rumors. Maybe he did it that way so that those who try to take over everything of value, leaving nothing for those who have so little, would not be able to find the real treasure. There were those poor evangelicals who, as well as for many others back then, were just a handful of men and women accustomed to the mocking and spitefulness of almost everyone else. But I didn't know that! The fact is that it had never occurred to me. I supposed they were embittered persons, who always closed themselves off in that big barn with gray doors and a strange front. I never imagined that they were the owners of the only real hope that remained in the village.

How wonderful it was to discover that in fact they were the truly triumphant people in our town! They taught me the truth. And not only with words but with deeds, the fruit of a sincere and unselfish love toward God and toward those who were lost like myself.

Village and Heaven

Could that be why we miss it so much? Is that the reason we never forget it? The train station is still there, although it is now used for something else. In many places where there was once a house, there is now only a distant memory. Only in a few places is there any evidence remaining of an older structure. And the people of yesteryear? The ones that are left leave the impression that they were caught unawares in strong winds, because they are bent over; some must walk with the help of sticks or canes, and on the faces of all of them passing time has left its mark. The stream that before seemed wide and strong, now seems so small and narrow that it makes you ask: "Is this the same stream or is it further ahead?" Its wide streets, desolate and clean, with no signs of life, invite illusions of a past that will never return. The school, the dreams, the teachers, the work places… everything has changed with the passing of time!

I don't think that what remains of the village is what I miss, but rather what is no longer there. The friends are no longer there, and nothing is the same! There only remain some memories of what was once alive. I believe that the entire picture leaves us with a great lesson to be learned. I think God allowed me to love my village so much, as well as my friends and my people, because he had a purpose. He wanted my mind to be filled with images, and then allowed it all to disappear, to be lost, to be destroyed, only to be transformed into a vast memory, just so that my heart would not remain there but rather to seek another place for its affection. I believe God did it to teach me something: that I might learn to not fix my sight or my heart on the things that are seen, since such things, when they no longer remain, leave an emptiness in the soul. And no heart can afford to live with memories alone! God wants us to set our sights on things above, on the things of heaven, for they are eternal, things that I will never lose.

So what was the purpose then of loving so much what I had to leave behind? It helped me to learn to love, to live out my dreams, to set down roots, to understand what is my real home, to be thankful, to desire re-encounters, to appreciate what is beautiful, good and pure. For heaven is full of those things that have been promised us. God taught me to long for that which I have not yet embraced through the simple things I have known in life. Isn't that an interesting idea! I know that reaching heaven will be like reaching my village after a long and hard day of work. That will be wonderful!

2.
The pathway, the farewell and a new beginning

*I*n that warm nest, made up of that old rough temple with a cement floor, those simple wooden benches, those brothers and sisters with a heart as big as a house and that old red piano accordion, I learned the first and unforgettable truths about God, Jesus, heaven, hope, faith and genuine love. There, beneath the shadow of those dear souls —trees that were truly planted by streams of living water— like Pastor Criollo and his wife Mary, I began to perceive the beauty of our great God. The days passed unhurriedly. Little by little, sin remained in the past, sadness was changed into joy and my life became so different that I began to think that I would never leave that place, for I would never be able to find another like it. And besides, who would want to leave all that behind?

"You must study", they said to me one day. "You must leave here and search for what God has for you. What you now have is worthwhile, that's true, but it is not even the shadow of what God has reserved for you. You must fly away and seek your place in the great work of God our Creator!"

God spoke to me clearly and through many others, and I decided to obey. I didn't ponder over the matter a great deal; I believe I didn't know well what I was doing, for if I had thought about it very much, I might never have left my village, my family and my congregation. God knew that! And the fact is that there was no real motivation to move; my family was going through the best time in their life and the church provided the best environment to achieve all those personal dreams that for various reasons had been relegated in my mind. But I decided to obey. And I thank God that I did!

A challenging path opened before me, and I started to move down that path carefully. I had no idea where it would lead me, but I knew very well who was accompanying me. So I responded: Yes, Lord!

There stood my mother that morning, on the street, standing next to the vehicle that would take me far away. She continued to wave Goodbye to me until we could no longer see each other. There also remained the dear brothers and sisters of my newfound faith, those whom I will always remember and to whom I will never be able to repay what they did for me. They always expected my return. They still await me. But I only returned to visit them and recount to them my experiences. I never returned to live and participate with them in that interminable and difficult struggle to remain faithful in the midst of so much resistance to believe in God, so common among those who live in small villages. Only God knows how much I have loved those brothers and sisters!

The pathway teaches us

A dead tree lying across the only path before you appears to be a great obstacle if your intention is to move through a dense forest. Your forward march is interrupted and you must resolve the problem as best you can. Your path must take another course, and the alterna-

tive route may seem at times a valid immediate solution, but a real problem later on, since it is easy to lose your way in the forest. People often lose their sense of direction in such instances. The noise, the lack of familiar signs and the monotony of the environment can easily confuse us, especially if we are inexperienced. A dense forest makes orientation difficult, and when the day is declining, the scene becomes more problematical.

To lose your path means lost time, even when later you find the way, and it could mean a significant loss if the proper pathway is not found again. Sometimes we can request help, but that is only possible when we encounter another person. For such reasons, we should not proceed along unknown paths alone and without a guide. But when there is no alternative, it becomes quite necessary to move slowly and carefully.

Loss of the pathway is always frustrating and worrisome, and can be rather dangerous in the midst of a forest, for we can become discouraged. Discouragement makes it more difficult to find again our proper path. Marching ahead is not the same when we face failure, fear and a sense of being lost.

This is the path of the believer: we move ahead easily in what we believe is the right direction; suddenly we are distracted, and when facing an obstacle we look for a shortcut or a path that seems to be the right one. Then chaos sets in little by little, and when we realize what has happened, it's too late. Better to return over the path we have taken thus far, but to do so requires that we be quite humble, and most of us are not that way. We usually assume that we can take advantage of the ground already covered, even when it has been the wrong path. We sometimes seek to resolve the problem by taking a shortcut that might lead us back to the right path; but the decision may be unwise, for it is like trying to fix one error with another. It is best to return by the path we have taken, recognize our error and begin again from the place where we made the detour. Although that may seem like lost time, it really is not, for it avoids other detours, teaches us to appreciate the right path and helps us to learn along the way. To learn the pathway well is wisdom that we need, if in fact we desire to reach heaven triumphantly.

A dead tree crossing our path seems to be a hard problem to overcome; but the same tree used as a bridge over a stream or a gully provides a solution to continue along the pathway. It would be like transforming the tree so that it becomes part of the pathway. Such is the life that God gives: we can turn obstacles into something useful when we give place to the Lord. Even that which is dead thus becomes useful. It is just a question of persevering. God knows we can do it. Let us not forget that Jesus said that only those who persevere to the end will be saved!

3.
Time to learn

*N*othing good or lasting can be done without knowing something; and when it comes to the Word of God, that is even more certain. The poverty I knew as a child did not allow me to study; I had to work hard in order for the family to eat at least once a day. The lack of basic knowledge limited me in my reading and understanding of God's Word, in spite of the effort I made to study it. The day finally came when I had to make some decisions about this; however unwelcome, it was not unexpected. I had to learn, even though it was costly to leave everything behind: the village, the brothers, the family and friends. I never stopped feeling my loss of them, and I doubt that I ever will. Those were long days of sacrifice; many days of hard work in matters that were new to me. They were times of studying everything I could possibly learn and of missing all that was familiar, even to the point of tears. The nights never seemed to end when I would dream of what I had left and felt the desire to return. Only God knows how many tears were shed on the path I had to take during those days in the seminary.

But nostalgia is not everything, nor can everything be seen as a trial, when we place ourselves in God's hands. In seminary you learn many wonderful things; you meet great servants of God, and it's also possible to find a good wife. I believe this stage was an advantage to me, for I acquired, with God's help, everything the seminary proposed for me. God helped me so much during this stage of life that my grades in all the subjects that I studied were the highest. That may not have been because of my ability as a student but because of God's mercy, for he knew that if I did not receive some extra encouragement, I would have returned to my village at the conclusion of the first year.

But God is good. Besides helping me to obtain the best that one can acquire in a seminary, he gave me a lot of loving and un-forgettable friends, real companions that even today, after all the years that have gone by, still stand by me in times of struggle. I always thank God for them.

Seminario

It was the longest trip I ever took! My friend struggled with his illness, trying to sleep in the seat at my side. But I couldn't even close my eyes. I could only think of what I had left behind. Outside, the dark night made the sadness that I felt the proper environment. Ahead, we could hardly see the road, with its monotonous signs. Only once in a while, the kilometer markers reminded me that each minute I was further away from all that I had left. Moving into the unknown was certainly not something very attractive.

The fear that some had awakened in me regarding the big city and its customs made me cling all the more to the few things I brought along: an old suitcase, a brief case and a guitar. These things were my entire earthly treasure, all that I had if I did not return to my village. I felt confused: I wept for what I had left behind, while my heart-beat indicated my anxiety. What did God have for me? How would my life be in the city? What enemies were awaiting me there? Had I been told the truth about the monster called The City? Would I fail? Would I triumph? Questions… lots of them. Answers… none. And the hours kept slipping by.

When I arrived, the hurried life of the city left me little time to think. The warnings given me didn't turn out as expected, and I had to make several urgent decisions. My friend almost didn't make it, and since I couldn't handle him as well as all the baggage we were carrying, I felt trapped by a sense of loneliness so scary that I could hardly bear it. But God continued at my side, just as he had promised! In spite of everything, I wanted to continue, trusting that perhaps what awaited me would be good for me.

After that came the first encounter, companions, the first class, the shared dormitory room, surprises, new friends, struggles, work, study and… Her! My companion, my sweetheart and the remedy for my loneliness! God had a chest full of treasures kept for me, and he allowed me to open it. So I did. I could hardly imagine all that was there! But among the anecdotes, tears, laughs, needs, work, study and other things, I discovered what God had for me.

If we serve God, we must do God's work. That being the case, what is only human is not always helpful. God must work seriously in us before we are really able to serve him, and that is painful and costly because it is God's work and not man's. We must let God do what he wants to do! That is easy to say and to hear, but it turns out to be very fulfilling, when we let God have his way in us.

4.
Back on the road

" If you study and don't share the knowledge gained with others,
all that you have learned will turn against you, and your
knowledge will become a stagnant pool". One of my unforgettable
professors said that, almost in passing, but it was precisely that
phrase that made me decide. So I got back on the road, which now
extended before me longer and more challenging than ever.

After traveling many hours through unknown scenes, I
wound up in the north of the country, trying to help a group of
believers that were facing difficulties. I stayed there almost a lifetime, working in every way I could, until I was able to mature a
bit.

Some day I will tell all that I lived and learned in those forgotten places, where I met many brothers of great value that I will
never forget. Like Hugo, my friend and companion in battle, to
whom I owe so much that I hardly dare write his name. And like
that other soul mate, dear brother Juan, a believer of absolute in-
tegrity, companion in prayer under the olive trees, one who knew
everything that a young man with a desire to be a servant of God
should know to avoid failing in the attempt. How will I ever repay
them? How can I remember all that I should? How can I name
some and not others? May heaven keep a proper register of all
that transpired! Entire lives dedicated to breaking through a heart
of stone; many years waiting for sweet and mature fruit for God;

people that knew how to teach with their life what one needs to learn to safely reach his goal.

My life is one of being helped and taught by many others. I have walked on paths that have left me with debts of affection and favors here and there. How could I fail to help others, when I always received help? How could I not be hospitable, when I have always been received as a guest? How could I not love, when I have received so much love? If I lived hundreds of years, I could not repay even a small part of all that I received in those unforgettable days.

Profound simplicity

Early in the morning, when the sun begins to reveal its rays of light on the meadow and the shades of night leave in a huff giving place to a new day; when the soul of simple men fully recover the hope of fulfilling their dreams in the light of the new day; when everything seems fresh and ready to experience; the day, the flowers and the birds contribute to that moment when it is delightful to look down the road, that narrow earthly ribbon full of years, that encourage men to move ahead and not be detained.

The road implies distance, and distance implies longing. To think of roads is to think of far away places, encounters, goodbyes and a thousand other such things. When we ponder a road we cannot keep our mind from going after some things. But we should not give too much credit to what appears at first sight; many things speak to us more profoundly when we take the time to open their treasures.

Almost no one gives attention to things that are quite simple. For example, who would dedicate a full hour to look at a road? Only someone who is melancholic or who misses greatly a dear friend who is gone. Or someone who has lost his wits or who is very sad and con-

fused. Most of us only use the road to reach the place where we want to go, and don't even keep track of it as we move along. But I think we should observe more carefully the simple things, for treasures are never hidden in very attractive places.

We need to keep in mind that while it is true that the road implies distance, it is also true that it implies proximity. The road is the pathway to the place where the person we want to see is waiting; it is the end of the trajectory; the road is also the place in which the march is begun. Every place is a road way. Road is the place where we set our foot before the trip begins, and it is not far from us, for it is here. It is the lack of assigning value to what we possess that makes us think that what is far away, or that what happens to others, is more important than what we have nearby, or that happens to us.

Jesus is great; he is impossible to see and understand, yet he is nearby and he is simple. So simple that when he is here, he doesn't call attention to himself. So simple and humble, that we pass him by. But someone who stops to look carefully will discover that nothing is more profound or interesting than he.

Perhaps that is the reason that many seek him in sophisticated ways without finding him. Maybe that is why many await him from heaven, and feel that he is late in coming. Many cry out for his visitation, and do not understand that he is at their side, under them, for he is the road. He is the road on which we walk each day. He is the wine and the daily bread. This is the simplicity only understood by children, poets, those who are in love, the poor, the ignorant and the humble. They can see him and love him til they die, for they have nothing to lose, nothing to gain, nothing to say, nothing to question, nothing to claim, and nothing to investigate. For they lack everything and, because of that, they have time to look at the things that others don't see, such as a simple road. For that reason they are usually the ones that one day discover the treasures. The child believes everything that is told him; the poet observes what others would not ponder, and he sees beauty that others do not expect to see; those who are in love question nothing, nor do they doubt; the poor always settle for whatever is given them; the ignorant know almost nothing and don't question much; and the humble are meek, and they remain tranquil until the person who speaks to them is finished. That is the thing. There it is: the treasure is in that which is simple, hidden away where we walk.

Perhaps because you have not given value to the simple things you have not yet seen the Lord.

5.

Mountains, loneliness and return

*M*ountains are beautiful when you visit them as a tourist, or when you take a hike. But if you have to walk several kilometers on a continually ascending pathway, with a suitcase and accordion, they no longer seem attractive. Less so if the weather is very hot and you have no water to drink. I can assure you, in such circumstances you begin to feel rejection. The loneliness that you feel at such times is scary. Even more so when you miss what you have left behind. The emotion is more pronounced if you are a preacher without having chosen the occupation. But God is good and quite creative; he takes the little we give him and multiplies it and it always seems to be enough for everyone. In such places, far away and inaccessible, many people live and they need the gospel.

People need God, and they listened to what we told them, just as we had learned in the seminary. After repeating some phrases so many times, even we sometimes no longer believed them. But one day a miracle occurred: Someone believed and opened his heart to God. And you already know how God reacts when someone believes him. One was not enough, not even there, for he wanted to win others. God always wants to win one after another, for his love is for all. To win them is relatively easy and nice, but to teach them to follow… that's another story. The fact is, that is really difficult. More than difficult, I would say impossible for a young man who knows little, unless he counts on God's help, obviously. In such faraway places, I was also able to speak and help many who today follow Christ's footsteps in distant places around the world. Such as Raul, who has served the Lord in many different countries.

Sometimes that's the way you begin serving God: feeling impotent, lonely and often failing. Real loneliness is not just being literally alone; rather it is not being able to count on anyone even when many others are nearby. I think you feel real loneliness when you don't know what to say to new believers. That will teach you to pray! Those who usually run from prayer come to love it when the trials rage; they pray even when it is not their first impulse. Nothing is more effective in leading us to seek God than a new believer who wants to learn.

The days passed, and although I thought I would never leave, I had to return to the seminary where a quieter job awaited me and a sweetheart desirous of becoming a wife. Like myself, she had no idea what was ahead. The fact is that God chose us, one for the other, and prepared us beforehand for what was coming our way.

On one of those nights when I experienced loneliness and struggle, God inspired me with a song:

In the depth of my soul Jesus clearly wrote

With eternal pen and ink the word love.

Deep within my soul, that word was hidden away.

And if I don't discover it, it hardly seems to be present.

Lord, I pray that your help will always be near,

So that at each moment that lovely word I might discover,

That the love that you placed there might flourish,

That everyone might know, without being told, that you live in me.

After suffering so much in this world of pain,

I never realized that a simple word could have such value.

With the passing of time I understood that the word was indeed

Just what I needed to find happiness, and for my life to change.

Hear it!

If you want to serve God, you will become transcendent. If you become known for your acts of service, your life will change in unexpected ways. When you dream of serving, your dream is delightful; you feel encouraged and happy. At times your eyes wander to the horizon of your dreams. You are young and the path before you is just beginning. Everything seems possible and you feel that you are able to do anything. But you should know that after you begin, trials will surprise you. You must pass the exam that the Lord requires of all who want to walk with him. But do not fear, no one ever died because of that, and it is all for your own good, your own welfare. God understands that what happens in the world is evil and he wants to prepare you to face it. Our gracious God will take your hand and show you that what is written is true. He will enable you to practice the theory. Don't worry about the trials, move forward with determination and courage. Better to be concerned about those who want to see you fall, those who criticize you. They are cruel, for they don't want your triumph to remind them of their failure. They cannot bear that your boldness reveal their fear. Nor that your decisiveness should threaten their dominion. Perhaps it is even more important that you be careful when you are applauded. Such applause can be even worse, for their praises can cause you to trust in your own strength; that is not convenient for those of us who serve God, for when we think that we have it all figured out, we will surely fall into something unexpected.

Just bow your head, look at the road and move forward. The pathway will offer you all that you need. And if you do that, one day, after a while, you will look around and not be able to believe all that has occurred while nothing was lacking. I know what I'm talking about!

God says that those who observe the wind will not sow, and those who watch the clouds will not harvest. That is to say, if you worry about the problems and struggles that you must face, you will lose your courage.

6.
Two that are now one

*T*he best. Really the best. Who but Carmen would have put up with so many mistakes and failures on my part. We married in the month of May, poor like the poorest, but full of illusions and dreams. We had no honeymoon or dinner the first day we were married. But God was with us and filled us with his presence and love. Right away we began to labor together intensely in the Lord's work, overtime every day, without holidays or Sundays. We often returned home on foot, for we walked a lot. Nothing could stop us, neither cold nor heat, in the work and struggles of those days. It all served to help us grow and learn, so as not to fall into the unseen traps hidden in life.

God is amazing! His lessons are not as academic as some say or would like for him to be, but he is the best teacher; he always manages to "pull some rabbit out of the hat." We were just two poor little chicks, with the illusion of being God's servants, but God's great mercy sustained us and he never despised our ideas and plans, even when they were full of imperfections. And we continued to have an open house to receive everyone that we believed God was sending our way.

After a while came a great victory over loneliness: God gave us a "quiver" full of children. We would never again be alone. And since we have been able to make progress when there were only two of us, we felt that with such an abundant household everything would be better. In reality, children are a gift from God, a very special gift. Our home filled up with new sounds, new languages (somewhat ill-spoken), new life and, of course, with new hope and responsibilities as well. We wanted them to grow up healthy; we wanted to educate them in the Lord's way. And even beyond the innumerable mistakes we made, that is what we did, and what we still do. We can never repay the Lord for the joy we have, knowing that all our children are serving him.

Carmen

«Some day I will do something significant for you», I said to her one day. She smiled, as always, after listening attentively to my crazy ideas.

«You have already done a lot for me», she responded.

The years passed, leaving a trail of anecdotes, struggles and triumphs. I have sought often to pay that debt, but I have been unable to do so. What could I do for someone like her? How could I pay for so many years of good will and faithfulness? I haven't even learned the proper way to thank her, although I have thought about it a lot.

She is like a fountain of cool water on a hot day; water offered with love, in a clean vessel, in the shade, while listening to delightful music. She is like a friend in times of loneliness and trial; a caring friend that says nothing out of place, that does not bother or demand anything in exchange for her company. She is like a gentle rain; a soft summer shower, when you are away on a vacation, looking through a broad window at a beautiful and colorful park as the rain comes down. She is like a page of paper; a blank page at your side, just where you would first look when you feel inspired and want to write something down. She is like a fertile meadow; fertile in every sense, with broad and immeasurable generosity, on a sunlit morning, after a light frost; while taking a pleasant walk on a clean path, with the aroma from a fresh rain. She is a simple woman, but one whom God, for some unknown reason, filled with an uncommon prudence, a wisdom seldom seen and simplicity worthy of a wild flower.

Tomorrow, when the sun comes up, she will be a year older, and will expect a surprise that perhaps will not come… I don't know! Fellow Christians will come to greet her. The children will be at her side early, like recently cut flowers; she will rejoice when she sees them, even when one is lacking for the complete bouquet. The day will pass with gifts, and greetings; and then things will settle down. Which means that she will put on her simple work clothes, care for the children and disciples who are on their way to heaven, offer me help in everything, pray, struggle, laugh a little, work hard and wait.

As I write, I am thinking that perhaps I should not do any of the things that I proposed to do for her. God says that a person's deeds are not to be paid twice, and God pays better than I. I believe that what I should do is not to be earthly but heavenly and eternal. I should not mess up with my own vanity all the treasure that she certainly has in heaven.

7.
God has his own school

G od knows from the beginning what is going to happen. He is
not limited like us who can only know partially what is happening now. He is kind and never makes his children take subjects
that will later be meaningless. He knows how to take advantage of
everything that happens to us, all that we do and all that we learn.

There were times in our life, and this is one of them, when we
have had to face unthinkable trials, go through times when we felt
we could not come out well from the enemy's trap. Unexpectedly
and without mercy, there appeared before us problems that
seemed impossible to solve, problems we had never experienced,
that made us feel that we would not make it through to the other
side. At times, when everything seemed to be going well, unimag-
inable difficulties surprised us, that seemed to have no possible
explanation. But God already knew that of which we were completely ignorant; he knew what we would have to face later on.
And he was preparing us beforehand. And he did so very well. We
could not have imagined what the future would bring, so that at
that particular time the trials seemed incomprehensible.

Anyone who wants to serve and teach others to walk with
God must be willing to cry from time to time, since the Lord's
school is more practical than theoretical. The school functions as
you live. As you move forward, you learn. But even though at
times it is necessary to weep while you learn at the Lord's side,

nothing is more effective than his way of training you. Step by step, truth by truth, going over again as often as necessary when a subject has not been adequately assimilated. We do not pass the test until we really understand. God grants valid certificates and correct evaluations. He is never in a hurry, but he never arrives too late. Moreover, he never misses an appointment.

Without thinking!

There are things you would never do, if you only thought twice about it. There are places you would never go, if you were properly informed. There are words you would never speak, if you could know beforehand the results they would produce. But life is full of things we never thought we would do; places where we have never been; and we have often found ourselves facing the consequences of something we said without considering the consequences.

"I will serve you," he said one night long ago. "I will serve you wherever you choose." Sometimes we are very attentive and we feel that God is walking in our midst. And we are so happy with his company that without thinking much about it we say yes to everything we feel he tells us. That's what happened in the case just mentioned. That person remembers as if it were yesterday; the emotion and passion with which he tells the story are truly inspiring. Now the years have passed and anyone can see the result of the YES offered that unforgettable night. Truly God has blessed him! The struggle was fierce, the pathway risky, the barriers difficult. But today his arms cannot hold all the fruits that were harvested.

Those who know tell us that we need to weigh the matter carefully before launching out on a mission. And that is true. Better to plan everything with details before doing anything serious. Certainly God honors loyalty and obedience more than sacrifices presented to him by his children. Even the Bible recommends that we should be cautious before building towers and planning things.

But I doubt that David thought a great deal about facing Goliath. Nor do I believe that Daniel made many calculations before saying that he would not contaminate himself with the king's food. I suppose that Nehemiah did not have much time to consider the personal cost of rebuilding Jerusalem. If these and other such personalities had stopped to think beforehand what they might have to face, today we would not have the Bible.

Think about it and see whether you can resolve this apparent contradiction! I have tired to do so for a long time and haven't made much headway.

8.

A wise pastor

W hen you are facing problems, little is more useful than a wise pastor. Though we may know people who are well informed, none are equal to a person who has become a pastor through graduation from God's school. It is difficult to go very far if you don't have a pastor who cares for you and can guide you aright. You may be able to walk on your own, if you have the strength to do so, but arriving at your desired destination will depend on a great deal of luck if you don't have proper orientation. Anyone who finds a good pastor that he can trust finds a real treasure.

God planned the church to get people back on track. Pride and sin not only take us away from God, but also separate us from others. And many of us, before we turned back to the Lord's house, had a disordered life, jumping from one impulse to the next, alone, facing like Quijotes the bitter experiences and barriers hidden from view at every step. But when you return to God, you aren't wandering around any more for now you have someone to counsel you whenever you are at a crossroads. That is why God gives us pastors!

The Lord reserved for us a pastor who was able to guide us rightly, even in the years when the work was very hard. A person who was determined to bless those ideas that others could hardly understand. A pastor who has not changed through the years, and whose concern continues to be the same as on that first day.

The unity of the church, the body of Christ, is more than a nice idea. It is not simply theoretical. It is a very practical matter requiring perseverance, responsibility, consistency and faithfulness. There are times when it is difficult to maintain unity. But thankfully there are people who do not give up, who overcome obstacles and keep moving in spite of everything, seeking God's will in this matter. Those men will always be there, just where God placed them.

For Hugo Baravalle

It was a sunny summer afternoon, now long past, but still as current as today's newspaper. A city with a strange name, the path, the park, the buses, that unknown place and, finally, the house. The encounter had been planned for business reasons; but God had rather different plans. And at the conclusion of the visit, there were no more doubts. Instead, there was a project for the extension of God's kingdom.

When you have been raised in an unrestrained environment it is not easy to live in a different way; something doesn't seem right. I remember that when I was a child, my mother raised chickens. To keep them from getting out of the pen and getting lost, or caught by predators, she would cut their feathers. That worked well, since with their wings cut they couldn't fly; and since they could not fly, no chickens were lost. With such a lesson I learned that with your wings trimmed you cannot fly. When the time came to serve God, I tried in different ways, but almost always some big scissors cut back my longing to fly. Inhibited in this way I reached your home that afternoon: without wings, but with a great desire to fly.

That afternoon you taught me that no one can really live a free life if he doesn't learn God's truth. Without truth, there is no freedom. And if there is no one to teach you with love and care, you will not be able to effectively learn the truth. These and similar lessons are what I owe to you, and I believe that I will owe them throughout my life, for how can such a debt ever be paid?

With the passing of time we have been able to win some victories. Faith opened the way through fear and the feathers began to grow again, my soul was healed, and God was often glorified, for the freedom that was gained was useful for me, for my family and for many more.

So here we are, hoping that our wings will grow until they are like yours. Ah... your wings! They are so large they make me envious. I have learned that under them I can find shelter in times of doubt, or when a child is lost, or when hurt is real, or when I am alone or face temptation. Your wings are truly blessed!

I offer to you this, my humble homage marked by the sweat of harvests that were costly, tears of departure, the loss of dear brothers who have gone to heaven, disciples that were under hell's sway but who are now workers, and many who have been restored for God's praise.

9.
Family and dreams

*M*y wife and my children have helped me to live and to keep dreaming. I was always a dreamer, with dreams impossible of fulfillment. Since childhood I have shared with enthusiasm my "fascinating ideas," but because they were so difficult to carry out, no one gave me much attention. Besides, they almost always involved plans to be carried out in cooperation, so they ended in failure. For that reason I always felt like a dreamer who was unappreciated.

As well as I can recall, all through life I have tried to help others. Most of my time was dedicated to others, rather than to myself. And since my help never seemed to be appreciated, there were times when my frustration left me with little desire to continue. Before I was a believer, that made me very sad; but later, after an encounter with God, I learned that it was better to not receive earthly recompense, nor gratitude or applause, I learned to appreciate God's recompense for those who help others. I soon learned as well that in the Christian life we must go through trials and come out of them approved, for with such experiences one can aspire to certain benefits that God reserves for some of his children. Such truths are not learned in any other way except by living at God's side and learning to trust him. So I began to get valuable lessons from every difficulty that I had to face. I hardly realized at the time that later all these experiences would be useful for the ministry.

The family was always the workshop for my ideas. They welcomed each thing that occurred to me to make things a little better: improvements and expansions in our home using materials that nobody else would use, sophisticated ways of increasing our meager income, original toys formerly unknown and entertaining pastimes that were unbelievably economical. All were received with joy and gratitude to God. Over time those small accomplishments encouraged us to help others, for we realized that imagination accomplishes more than money and is also quicker. God always helped us to see in everything that we received the solution that we sought for some of those whom we needed to help.

All these things were done without expecting recompense or gratitude, for my family has learned very well that it is better to not receive gratitude from anyone, so that the payment for the good that was done for others might be transformed into heavenly treasure.

The children

The silence is confusing. The home is empty. David's strong voice is missing, where he usually fills the place with sound. Florencia's shouts are missing, such as when she is playing in the patio with her friends. Marisa's music is not there; although the most monotonous I have heard, it is still inspiring and profound. Elias' noisy work is gone, as well as the rustling pages of a book, read over and over. Neither is there any noise from the scissors and other school supplies of Gabriela while she prepares a lesson. Sarah is also missing. The children are not at home. Each one is away with his own activity: walks, retreats, and even one is talking with God, face to face.

It's hard to live without them; I miss them a lot. The hours pass more slowly; we anxiously await their return. We have spent our life surrounded by innocence, strange questions, recently invented language, abundant caresses, and moments filled with joy. We are one of God's families, and we have always served him, do so now and will continue to do the same.

Carmen is fixing supper. I have a gift for each one. The telephone rings and interrupts us, but what we hear simply opens a parenthesis in our thoughts. We are rich. God has filled our home with children — more than that — with children that love what we love, and do what we do; they struggle every day together with us and they await Jesus' return, just as Carmen and I do.

The noise appears again. They have arrived! We go out to receive them. There are hugs, questions, hunger and weariness. With one hand they receive the gift and with the other, supper. Those who talk the most tell us of their experiences. And then off to bed. We look at each other, across the table, satisfied with what we were able to do to make their homecoming interesting, perhaps so that it will never cross their minds to not return at some point, for life would be without meaning apart from them.

10.
The first disciples

O bedience was required, and the order was to make disciples. The pastor's counsel was quite clear, and could not be avoided. The truth was before our eyes, ready to be practiced; we only had to get started. In theory, it all seemed easy to understand and to carry out successfully, a complete project. But when we began to put it into practice, it turned out to be quite difficult. The same truths that for us were valuable discoveries, to our discipleship candidates they sounded like words of an unknown language. And no matter how hard we tried, we were unable to get them to understand a single syllable. But, as always, here again the Lord came to our rescue and in time everything changed. The result was truly abundant and nothing was lost. Preachers often tell about the burdens, the treason, the disappointments and the ingratitude they receive from people they try to help move the ministry forward. For myself, as I recall the first "victims" of my newly found "ministry," I feel like I would like to look them up to ask their forgiveness. Those first attempts to lead people to God were so confusing that our new congregation looked more like a small group lost in an immense forest than a group of Christian disciples.

But God was good to us and helped us to come out all right and to learn something every day; a little of all that must be learned to carry out this eternal job of making real disciples of Jesus. When he underscored the benefits of making disciples, the pastor I mentioned told me that only by forming many of them could I reach the objectives that I felt I should achieve. And so it was, for several of them are now workers that are moving forward the work that we do for God. We have never stopped being or making disciples for Jesus. Nor do we even think of that as an option.

Trappings of a poor boy

"Is it true that Jesus will return to get us?" he quizzed firmly, as if he really wanted to say: "You know what will happen if that isn't true!"

What a daring question! How could someone who calls himself a Christian ask such a question? It seems obvious that we must believe what Jesus said. But I should be grateful to God for having learned that to respond to questions in the right way, you first have to understand them. Sometimes people ask a question which encloses the truth they really want to understand.

"Jesus will return to seek his church!" I told him. And then added: "No one knows the day or the hour; but we do know that those who died in Christ will rise first, and then those who are still alive will be transformed to meet with the Lord." Then my mind got lost in a sea of data concerning that fascinating subject.

The perplexed look on the face of the boy bothered me, I must say, since it kept me from concentrating on what was obviously my theological exposition concerning the Lord's return. And as I recognized my mistake, while still talking, I sought in my mind for the simplest way to communicate those truths. Yet he seemed to understand nothing of what I said.

Suddenly, in one of those intervals that are real blanks, those sensations you sense when you don't know what to say or how to say it, he spoke again and reformulated almost the same question as at the beginning. Now it seemed that I was the one who didn't understand.

"Is Jesus coming to look for me… really?"

Extreme innocence of someone who had never had anything, and who now began to have faith in something he had never seen. Desires for someone to come who had been delaying for many years. A heart weary with so many "going aways" and abandonements, that cried out for someone to return. An ear so accustomed to hear bad news that it had grown impatient before the possibility of receiving some good news.

"Don't worry about that anymore, son," I said. "Let's make it simple: If it were not the truth, your faith and my faith would make it true. I promise you! Jesus will come back to seek you!"

When you don't know what to say, but you must help others with words, always grab some surprising resource that you didn't even know you had. I assure you; it works!

11.
We can win others!

We knew very well that we were persons that the Lord had rescued from the trash heaps of this world. And the same as Carmen and I, those who began to understand the message also came from a background of much suffering. Although it was difficult to help them and teach them, the small group that came together was united, with a desire to serve and filled with gratitude. Most of us came from families that were messed up or troubled and we came into the church like someone grasping for the last straw. We had almost all wasted our years in vanities, and now we needed to live in a different way, if we expected to recover or change our lives. God had called us as we were, and through many ups and downs, struggles and decisions, he was getting us back on track. Our life was being built with the truth and we could work, study, restore our families and take the right path. And we were even encouraged to begin to do some significant things in our service for the Lord.

Of course, since it could hardly be any other way, the things we did were different from what most Christians did. We were happy families that God had rescued and built up, and for that reason we began to think that we should do something more for those who were still unacquainted with the Lord's truth. One day we realized that others were listening to us. That enthused us and we decided to serve the Lord full time, with all our strength and our whole heart. We felt we could never stop. And when we stopped to take account, the work had grown quite a bit for us; it was beyond our ability to handle in every area. We had to work hard, day and night, to keep from losing the value of what we had found.

God is good! Our store of grain is still full with part of what we harvested during those difficult times.

To speak for those who cannot speak for themselves

Who will speak for those who cannot speak for themselves? Who will defend the oppressed? Who will fight for those who have already lost the battle?

It was hard to overcome individualism with solidarity and favor; these qualities have withdrawn into small places, afraid of dying. As a rule, each person seeks his own; most people only think of themselves. In a few full pockets is found that which many lack. A few enjoy plenty; and most live with very little. Sadness beats its chest in the parks and the streets. It's like the ancient giant Goliath who has returned, shouting defiantly against those who struggle with it. Most people tremble when they hear it in the distance. Hiding away in the refuges that still remain, they hope to be saved without understanding what it is they fear. Their pride only allows them to think of themselves. They dream that when the unknown comes, that perhaps before the rest, they can find some way out. Their desire is that what they hope for will not delay, that it won't be too hard to discover, that it will be free and that it won't require much effort to obtain. They don't realize that to hope for the unknown is vain. Whoever does not know what he is waiting for will never be happy. Anyone who does not work to achieve the victory he longs for will never be satisfied.

I am responsible! If I recognize what is happening, then I am responsible. Even if I don't have strength, I am responsible by virtue of the fact that I know a little more. Or because I have heard what God says.

We have to go into the streets and say to the weak and to those who are defeated to give up their refuge, that they not surrender to death without a struggle. They must fight, they must believe that history can be repeated, that the world is awaiting another "David" to conquer that "Goliath" who has come on the scene. Many look out through the windows of their hiding places, and when they see a small person who is willing to fight the giant, they will come out of their caves and help.

There are many who hardly speak, because no one has ever listened to them, but who are delighted to tell us their beautiful dreams if we are ready to listen and to speak for them before the ones who should be listening. And if we speak, others will hear us, for they will be surprised by the things we tell them. Who doesn't want to listen to something interesting? Some will listen out of mere curiosity, and will be surprised when they understand what we are saying. Others will give us their attention in order to accuse us later, for reasons unknown to us. But there will be some who hear us and help us to achieve something for many others. That's the way it is. I have seen it!

Even God considers that it is important that we speak for those who don't speak for themselves! Prayer is proof of that. God taught us to ask for those who don't know how or are unable to do so, by calling us to intercede in prayer for others.

12.
Treasures in the garbage

*D*ue to my upbringing, I learned a lot about treasures that are often found in the garbage heap. As a child, the only valuables I knew about were things that others threw away. My mother discovered there essentials to raise us, from cloth to make diapers, to toys, and a lot of other items that she was able to sell to provide food for the table.

When you don't have anything, you can usually find what you need by looking through the things others have discarded. Many throw things in the trash that they no longer find useful, and with some imagination you can transform what you find into something useful. That is a reality unknown by most people, but it is the way of life for many today.

The people that heard our preaching were poor, very poor. Some had no home and we had to do something for them. The situation gave rise to some doubts, for many warned us that the openness of those recently converted was not sincere but simply a maneuver to get some money through the help that we could give them. "What money?" I asked myself a thousand times. Sincerely, we could not believe that someone could use a sophisticated hidden maneuver to obtain our "extraordinary capital." Who would want our poverty? On the other hand, we figured that none of them had any reason to think in a sophisticated way.

One day, after meditating on the different opinions that we had heard, we decided to put our "money" at the disposition of the poor people who had most recently come to us. The capital involved lasted barely a week. But we realized that they had not come for money but for Jesus' love, for they had found in him the escape they needed. Great! Now we had a small congregation, made up of those whom very few wanted, to whom we needed to give our attention.

But God had a good idea, and it had to do with the garbage. We started with wood, metal, bottles and other waste products. Then other valuable things were added that got transformed into houses, furniture, tools and food for those that we wanted to help. In time we learned that in the garbage heap you also find people. God showed us that people who had been discarded by others are really precious jewels that can be recovered. How many we have seen coming from such a background! How many of them are now valuable in every sense of the word! Many of them now adorn heaven! How we thank God for having encouraged us in all this!

Simply Miguel, that's all!

One day he came to our house. It could have been any day, a lifetime ago. He came for no reason, and had nothing with him. A torn leather bag hung from his shoulder, the strap crossing his chest and back. I had never smelled anyone like him, and no one spoke the way he did. He was hungry and ate everything he could get; even the food left in the plates of others. His clothing was worn and dirty, and his beard was gray and unevenly cut. All this made him the most mysterious man I had ever seen. He spoke of profound wisdom, travels to faraway places, exotic customs and ancient religions. He said he was Jewish and in the process of recognizing Jesus as the Messiah. He stayed until nighttime. Then he returned the next day, and the next and the next. Finally he stayed to live with us. And eventually he got into the heart of us all. He became our brother when he was baptized. Then he became the friend of most and the uncle and grandfather of many. He was and always will be for us "the Jew." There will never be another like him. A day ago, or maybe a month ago, I really don't know how long, he went to be with his Messiah, to ride on clean clouds. He became tired of the filth here and he left rapidly, almost without saying goodbye. He won't return. He stayed there; obviously, he liked heaven and he stayed. The fact is that Jesus always wins us over; he knows how to treat us well and his dwelling places are better than our farmhouses.

The rest of us stayed here: some of us still not understanding his life style, others criticizing his faith and faithfulness to God, others trying to understand his interpretations of the Bible. But ourselves… we were simply amazed! How great it will be when we arrive and find you, you old character!

How wonderful if we could see you surrounded by children, shooting arrows with your bow and distributing candy. How great it would be to wake up and discover that it was only a nightmare and that you are still living. But it's true! You left. For it not, you would have collected the debt of those at your side… and several days have passed without any claim from you.

How amazing! More and more we find ourselves missing certain personalities. The lovely old character with the crazy dreams, the hard-nosed business man with the broken sandals, the manufacturer of the most exotic knives, the guy in love with Israel, that lived far away to avoid messing up his land. Some day we will meet again, and then, yes, everything will be clear and beautiful. Nothing will keep us from talking a long time about what we like without anyone bothering us. Wait for us, brother, for we will meet again!

13.
If you have nothing to give, you can love

The love for our children helped us develop our faith and imagination; when we had nothing to give them, we never said: "There's nothing…" We prayed and obtained, whatever the cost! That method, applied on a greater scale, has always given us results when we needed to help others. I believe with all my heart that love is a miracle; if we really love someone, the same love that we experience will enable us to do something for that person. I doubt the assertion of some who say they have great love for someone and yet they only manage to achieve their own satisfaction, even though they say they love with passion. You could also doubt the love professed by those who preach, counsel and teach about love, but never show it in their deeds.

If there is a way to show love other than giving away something valuable that we posses, I don't know what it is. It is true that I am not very well trained in theological matters, but it doesn't seem very hard to understand this point. I believe that God's word shows clearly that we should express something that shows what we feel. The most important thing is not to try to convince others about what we think, but allow others to see and experience God's love through the things we do. To allow that love that we have received to express itself freely until the miracle occurs of putting our hands in movement, while expecting those signs that the Lord promised to those who believe. We only need to dedicate our lives to Christian love, and we will then discover what to do as we love.

It was not easy to come to believe this way in my life. And by thinking in this way, a lot of doors have closed to me forever.

A certain day I went to a retreat of church leaders that developed into what we call a "pastors' getaway." During the meetings everyone talked about the nicer things in their ministry. I had only been recently recognized as a pastor and had come to the encounter full of doubts and questions, for I found myself at a real crossroads. I had heard a thousand voices in recent days and their messages confused me: "You are not doing the right thing," "You won't get very far with that kind of people," "It's hardly worth while to dedicate so much time and effort to obtain so little," "Leave that group and start to work with a real ministry." Those and similar phrases kept me from discovering what was correct. I wanted to take off running from that retreat, for all that I heard there was urging me to make decisions. And even though I was becoming accustomed to working with the poor, I didn't want to fail God, if he really expected something else from me. A few hours later, in the shade of some trees, I could clearly hear God's voice saying to me: "Omar, you are sick. Go where you find the poor. They will heal you." After getting over the shock of hearing that, clarity came from the Lord and then comprehension and finally obedience. After that experience, I returned to the meeting hall knowing that I was the pastor of the poor that the Lord had given me to care for. I had no more doubts. God had resolved my problem of identity and placement in his great work.

A Secret story!

The silence confuses me. It is very early on Monday morning. And another week of struggles begins. The quality control in my mind discards one by one all the ideas that occur to me. The hours pass rapidly. The day begins again; and with it the enemy returns to attack. Of course he does! It never fails. He always comes, and with strategies much better than those of yesterday. While most are still sleeping, he waits in his hiding place. When others awake, he will attack with destructive fury.

It's dark. A little soldier thinks and thinks: How could I do my job in a better way? How should I lead the attack in order to overcome? How can I be more effective? Another, who only obeys orders and doesn't need to think so much, is sleeping. Near his post, a third is on guard duty next to the fire. Beyond him, another looks at the stars, as if imploring God's help. Night and day, from one Monday to the next. Without a break. No rest. Without stopping to think about themselves. They live that way most of the time. They are the soldiers in God's army, those who fight against hunger here where it is my lot to serve the Lord.

Almost all of them have the same characteristics: they come from situations that are hard to understand. They speak very little about their job. They are ingenious; they have become accustomed to miracles. They are constant, resistant, responsible and clean; and they are well trained to get along with what they have. This is because they have been formed in specialized training camps, where the refrigerators make more noise than in other places because they have very little inside. Where in the kitchen cabinets there are only empty bags that once had food. Where the jam and jelly jars, for whatever reason, never seem to have anything. And where the bread bag is just an adornment. They come from places where the people sit at the table waiting for what never arrives and they make do with what there is.

Places where people eat little food and say such things as: "At least there is something," "What can we do?" "Tomorrow will be another day," and similar phrases.

The time arrives, the sun comes up, everyone awakes; the children's stomachs make their presence known. They are the first ones attacked by this enemy, one of the most terrible and most feared: hunger.

I write in order to encourage the army. Or rather to honor them, for I don't think they need more courage. Perhaps I write to avoid staying outside, to participate with them in some way, to be one of them.

All right, let's go! That's enough writing for now, we must put our shoulder to the wheel! The movement outside begins to make noise. Some are selling, some are kneading dough, others cooking, and others go and come with things in their hands. We must hurry! Many are waiting for us with a clean plate, thinking that perhaps today the meal will be abundant and there will be dessert... Perhaps!

14.
The poor help the poor

The first thing we started in the town of Rafael Castillo was a Bible school. We did so with the desire that many might learn God's word. It was the poorest school anyone could imagine. And as I mentioned earlier, almost at the same time we began with the first group of disciples, where the principal characteristic was that we chalked up more mistakes than successes. At the same time, on a very simple scale, we started a community "soup kitchen." Next came a more numerous congregation, in which the disciples from the street and the surrounding darkness quickly became the most prominent participants. Then the farming projects, and everything involved with that, such as construction teams, workshops, small factories and other commercial enterprises. As the years passed, it all became what is now known as Adulam.

To be poor is a little like finding yourself in the midst of a labyrinth without a guide or instructor, facing the pressing urgency to find a way out, while alone. This describes, more or less, the history of most of those who got involved with us. Because we had no money to share, we thought that since God had taught us how to get out of our own labyrinth, we could make rescue operations from time to time to find those who had a real desire to be free. We would do it in the simplest way, just taking their hand and leading them to the exit. It seems easy to write this down, and easier still to talk about it. But it was hard to do, I can assure you. The person who is poor, because he has been in that desperate situation for so long, is unable to quickly understand that there is a reality different from the one he is living.

But it's not so hard to recognize those who suffer when you have lived in pain. It's not hard to walk down these paths, for if you want to, you will discover that you can do it. If we love God, we will be thankful for the way he has helped us. And that gratitude provides the motivation to work so that others can also escape from the web that has had them trapped.

Bread and fish!

When I am before you, Lord, I always feel worthless. Besides that, I have nothing worthwhile to offer you, for I possess nothing. An entire life of work and more work and all I have earned is a few fish and some bread. Of course, I watch over them carefully, since they are my only earthly treasure. I am always giving, but I only give away something; I never want to remain empty handed.

But today is different! You have won my heart again. Today I will give you my bread and fish. The fact is I was tempted. The merchant that is always hiding within me came out of his cave. He heard about the great opportunities for investing in your kingdom, and cannot resist. Everything goes! Just like you want it. I want to give you everything! Of course, what I have is not all that much; I already told you that I never had much. Worse yet, I am now older and more battered. I know that if you give me a hand, I can stand up again, and with your help I will do something. It will not be like when I was young, but I don't expect to bring you shame.

Today I brought my five small loaves and the two fish I have left. I want to see how you will feed all those who are around me, as well as all those who are coming, for there are many. I know that I am not like the boy in the Bible, for when he gave you his bread and fish he didn't know what you would do with them, and I do know. And it may be that I am selfish as I give them to you, for I know that I am not going to lose anything. But please receive them. After all, if my intentions are bad, I will lose everything, and your only loss will be a little time. But if we win, everything will be yours. All I ask in exchange is that you never allow me to remain apart from what you are doing. Does that seem like too much to ask?

What do you want me to do? I cannot find a way to give you something without being the first one benefitted!

15.
Practical love

S ince the people kept coming to our meetings from the strangest places, and usually with almost nothing, we had to do something practical for them. We knew that Jesus had spoken quite clearly about the needy. We had learned that we had to give something to those in need because, whichever way you study it, God's word shows us that, and it needs to be applied literally. It was not a question of interpreting the Word as we chose, nor consider it as an allegory, a parable or symbolism; whatever the Lord said on this subject had to be read and applied directly. No need to go around the "mulberry bush." And if you understand it that way, but don't have money, you will surely seek God and the miracle will occur. At least that has been our experience.

Little by little, in the simplest way imaginable, the storage barns began to appear, as well as houses, vehicles, and everything else this work of God required to function. Of course none of it was new, nor the best quality, but everything was useful. One day the first pickup truck arrived, which we were anxiously awaiting, to the point that all of us were out in front long before the scheduled time it was to arrive, to see it and to relish in the result of our faith. When the moment came, we spotted from a distance a new yellow vehicle, which turned out to be the one carrying our pickup. As it came closer, I didn't know whether to look at the faces of the believers, now transformed by frustration, or the junk that was arriving. It was the most broken-down pickup imaginable, as if someone had messed it up on purpose. It was also more than old; it looked like the first one of that brand that had been manufactured. We were never able to fix it up and, of course, we never got it to run. But it served to humble us and helped us to learn to wait on God. And to learn to pray, so that we would understand that it was God who gave us things and not our own achievements, as we tried to answer for ourselves the prayers, rather than wait on God. Eventually, even the pickup bore its fruit.

Love for the work and for the brothers and sisters, who were now increasing in number, enabled us to continue happily moving forward in our small Citroën. So much so that, even though it was an automobile for four persons at the most, we used it for as many as twelve. We learned that it was easier to push a car to get it started when several were traveling in it.

We always gave thanks to God for what we had, and that attitude helped us to keep in mind what God had determined for us. Moreover, it prepared our hearts for the prosperity that came in time.

A story without shoes

"Wait until tomorrow. Mamma will come earlier and will bring you what she promised."

She said it again and again, and after a while her voice became more convincing, as if she had already found the solution. I watched them without their taking notice. On one side, the little fellow who was seeking shelter in that new personality that he called "Teacher", who had appeared in his life a few days ago and who seemed to have authority over him. And on the other, that small and bold apprentice learning to serve God, who pretended to fight without weapons against the giants that dominated the lives of children in the poor neighborhoods. Perhaps that morning we would learn that the tears that are hardest to overcome are those that are timid and silent, for they always come from old and deep wounds, sometimes inherited.

How can someone develop hope when he has never experienced it? How can you explain it to someone who has never known it? It's easy to preach about hope before those who already have hope. But it's not the same when you try to induce hope in someone who has never had it. For some reason God said that he would produce in humans both the desire and the deed according to his good will. God doesn't come to us without bringing the solution. He knows that when a person falls, he is no longer capable of having hope. Those of us who speak of God should keep these truths in mind, for we find ourselves frequently with those who have lost everything, even the desire to escape from their unheard-of situations.

But children are children. Evil has not yet totally trapped them, and we can always find some resource that we can use to help them to understand the truth. Imagination can be a great tool. A child, regardless of how poor and abandoned he is, always retains something of that ability with which God has endowed every human being. Of course, if the one who approaches him doesn't also have some imagination, he will not be able to accomplish much. But those who preach to the lost are children of God; and can anyone be a child of God if he doesn't become like a child?

"Some day, when the time comes, the great God of heaven will gather around himself all the children that he has found out there; they will all be happy, and God will be happy too. You are going to go with him, riding on a cloud, and your mother will be with you. You will have new shoes and your friends will go with you."

The little girl who was preaching kept talking. To the point that suddenly her eyes began to shine as she looked toward heaven. Her account became more lively, as if she were telling of wonders that she was able to behold at that moment. "Don't worry too much about the shoes, — she said. — They don't use them in heaven. God is going to fill his heaven with poor children; and you are poor, a child and, in addition, good."

"God will take you with him, you'll see. What do you think, Yiye? How do you see heaven? Can you imagine being there? Maybe it's better now to practice walking without shoes, even for a little longer, to get ready. Up there you will always walk without them and, perhaps, God wants you to teach the children that never learned to walk without shoes. But you don't need to worry about thorns or rocks that hurt your feet, because God told me that there the streets are pretty and clean, and besides, they are made of gold."

16.
The first structure

e had to give some form to what had been accomplished. We found no other way but to structure and organize, even though we didn't know how to do it, since we still did not know of any other group that worked in a similar way to what had come about with us. Those who came to us were persons who are precious to God, and we had to teach and help them shape their lives. So we set to work diligently. We purchased a property. We got into debt. We organized retreats. We obtained other vehicles. And we developed a plan so that this new congregation could move ahead.

But when everything was almost ready to go, we faced the first small exodus of Christians who left us because they were not in accord with helping those on society's margins. It broke our hearts and almost ruined our plans. If earlier it seemed very hard to handle the expenses, now it looked impossible. We had to take drastic measures. And that meant that those of us who were left had to double our efforts, not only to pay the debts, but also just to move forward. It was just at that time that a need surfaced to help some who had been affected and abandoned because of AIDS, and that shot our budget to the skies. But the thing that was most difficult to resolve was the lack of workers; that alarmed us. The whole picture made us weary and elevated the demands on the majority of those who were left. Even so, joy over what we had accomplished and expectations for the future encouraged many of us to not abandon the work. We had to continue, in spite of the cost, and we did so.

When there are pastors that follow the divine mandate, everything is easier to carry out; and we were helped by the pastors that gave us oversight. They were nearby, making everything easier, paving the way in the legal aspects, and cooperating in whatever way they could. Finally, we developed a stable team to help, without ceasing to be the church of Jesus Christ for our region. God showed us that we should not try to take the place of the work that belonged to the government, nor take on tasks parallel to the public hospitals. Rather we had to carry out what he had shown us, which was to show love that no one else can give. That is, express God's love to the world by being the church. In that way God's purpose would also be fulfilled in those who had the least. We shall never be able to repay the pastors that helped us, and still help us with such love!

Shoulders… only shoulders are needed!

God's ark had to be carried back to its home. An enthusiastic king was ready to accept the challenge. Years of sin had caused the glory of God to depart from the people. Something had to be done! And it had to be done right. A caravan was prepared and a party that raised the enthusiasm of everyone. And in the excitement or not leaving anything to luck, a new cart was built to carry the ark; a cart pulled by two new and healthy oxen. Everything was ready!

The day arrived, and the journey began. Hearts burned with emotion awaiting the moment for the ark to arrive. Those years of waiting would not be in vain. Hope filled the spirit of everyone. But on the way there was a disaster, something no one expected. Maybe they were singing songs of victory too soon; perhaps something had been forgotten; they might have forgotten some detail, or didn't take something into account. How could they find out?

The ark could not be transported. Unexpectedly, the oxen did something strange on the way: the cart began to shake dangerously, and since the ark was falling, someone tried to sustain it with his hands. But it was not the right person, and he died instantly. Deep mourning filled the soul of everyone. What had gone wrong?

A person's intentions, or even that of many, may be very good. But God's work belongs to him, and cannot be carried out with good intentions, only with truth. It is God who determines the way and the timing. Moreover, he chooses the persons according to his sovereign will. We may have good ideas, but what God determines should be done the way he says. New carts are pretty, functional, comfortable and rapid. But God's ark had to be transported by Levites and carried on their shoulders. God doesn't yield an inch, nor by impulse, but by truth. The truth makes no room for questioning, no tricks, no short-cuts; truth is truth, one hundred per cent.

The ark of God had to be transported on men's shoulders, and not on a new cart. The same is true today: God's work is done so that people might know their creator, and while that is being done, those who do the work are also increasing their knowledge of him. It is not done on the new carts of comfort and human wisdom, but on the shoulders of men willing to give their lives to please God.

We should keep this truth in mind when we serve God, for he always acts in the same way. Just as he did before, he does today and will tomorrow. That which displeased him yesterday, does not please him today.

17.

Mistakes and horror stories

*G*overnment documents that were never processed; therapies performed incorrectly, out of ignorance; risks taken in vain; lack of wisdom in almost everything; too much suffering; erroneous counsel, given more than once; useless work done; unfulfilled promises... and a thousand other glitches filled our days, months and years. We always lived hoping for better times, without thinking a lot about our surroundings, in order to keep from getting discouraged. You get so used to such things that when something doesn't turn out badly, you fill like something is missing.

In the past, way back in time, there were those days. Some of those anecdotes we remember with humor and others with sadness; but all serve to improve the work we are doing and to keep us humble before God, because if he resisted us, we would collapse without remedy. We always regret that some have gotten mad or have despised us, thinking that we were building a new church, or developing a new life style, or trying to put into practice a new revelation. How we would like to have explained the truth to them all! Because the fact is that we were doing nothing new, except seeking to put into practice our faith in Jesus, just like the rest. We only wanted to eat every day and live like the rest, just as we learned from the Lord. And the only way we could do that was by acting as a community, and if we couldn't explain better that reality, it was simply for lack of wisdom.

Today everything is pretty well organized. We have gained some experience and knowledge. In addition, we have seen results, which speak better than words. But we continue to make mistakes, the most sophisticated and unusual errors that anyone could imagine.

In circumstances like those I have mentioned, we couldn't think about forming workers. The great effort expended, the pressure of having to pay accounts and services and the need of those that were coming submerged us in difficult and sacrificial work. We hardly stopped. We forgot to rest and we gave away everything: money, home, family and time. All just to save the greatest number of people we could. Precious lives, not physical property, were in the balance. We shall never know whether our choice was good or bad, or whether we made the right decision. We can only say that if we had not done that, we would never have known Ricardo, nor the Jew, nor Gloria, nor Tabera, nor Alejandra, nor Vaca... nor... nor...

Departures and returns

"Some day I'll return," he said, as if sentencing himself. Then he gave me a big hug and left. I said nothing, I'm not sure why. I've asked myself a thousand times, while watching him sink in the dense fog that for some time now has covered my days. When I could see him no more, I closed my eyes and tried to continue watching his rubber boots, his oversize worn-out pants and the gray bag hanging from his shoulder. He already knows that all of us are bad and sinners by nature; he already learned about salvation and the fact that all of us will give account to God. But the pain, vice and bitterness

that he has carried for so many years always wind up annulling his good intentions.

The only thing left is to try to fill the void he left; and that's impossible, or at least very difficult. The heart needs mending, since today it was broken a little more. That's the case each time this happens. Our mind searches and rejects, over and over, but nothing helps to get over the pain. Some day no one will leave!

I've also thought many times about leaving. Just leave... regardless of the destiny. Just like he did. He showed me that the first step is leaving, and then concern yourself with the destination. First comes the crazy idea of fleeing; then the uncertainty of having to start over again; after that, the sadness of missing what was left behind; later, the cowardice that doesn't allow us to return; and finally, the failure that, when all is said and done, is what overcomes all our pride and brings us back home. I know the list of steps well; I know what comes first, second, and on to the end. But I don't think I will try to leave again; and not because I don't want to live through those things again. It is rather that hoping, I learned to wait for it and discovered that it is more worthwhile to hope than anything else. I want to see him return, and I also want to see the return of others who, like him, left one day. God is gracious to respond to our prayers; and there is not a lot I need to do. Therefore I will stay and hope; I know that if I exercise faith and patience, I'll see them return.

That will be wonderful! There will be a thousand things to say. But I, at least, will say nothing. I'll just listen to what they tell about the path they took. I always have near at hand the water to wash their tired feet; and the water is always cool enough to quench their thirst. Seated together again on the tree trunks, we will feel that life is beautiful, that the opportunities are hands extended toward our friends, and that God's love crowns those who truly repent. Following that encounter we will be wiser than before. I'm sure of that!

I hope I won't be too old to run to meet them. I also hope that my eyes will still be able to see them when they return. I'm beginning to like the idea of waiting! My heart is filling more and more with hope!

18.
We didn't know the danger we faced

I don't know why, but we never perceived the danger faced in God's work if we didn't develop workers. Perhaps we were warned, but because of so much work, we didn't pay attention. Maybe we knew, but we didn't develop them, and we really didn't know how to do it.

One day when a pastor visited us, he mentioned two things in that regard: "This work must go through the test of time," and "God has shown me that you need to recycle, just recycle. Recycle the persons, just like you recycle the things that others give you."

God spoke to us through that concerning the fact that we suffered through many trials and he indicated that we should try to get through them in victory, applying what we had learned. So that is what we did.

When we turn to the Lord, we discover what we did wrong and what we need to learn. Yet we certainly went through some tough times, when we thought we would sink. We may have given the impression of being negligent, or closed to counsel. Or that we confided in ourselves and left things to pile up. But the truth is that I often did not know what to say to the workers or what to do next. In any case, we did the best we could. At times we wondered about all that we did not know, rather than bother the pastors who gave us oversight. And if we acted like we were happy, it was because we really were happy, even as we served God in the midst of society's castaways. Maybe we didn't know how to communicate to others what we were really going through; perhaps our mistake consisted in not wanting to make known the reality of our troubles and needs.

We always tried to keep a positive attitude and we gave testimony to encourage those who listened, because it seemed the right thing to do. Perhaps if we had done things differently it would have worked out better. However, the truth is that the Lord showed us that he didn't call us to enjoy human successes, but to preach and obey; and we have tried to do that the whole time.

There have been times when, suddenly and without warning, a string of mistaken assumptions, small mistakes and rumors clouded our skies, filling them with dark and threatening clouds that shook us up. But the Lord always showed us something fresh on every occasion. I laugh when I remember those times! Often we had no idea what to do with all that faced us!

Danger is ever present. The risk we assume means that we often face tough times, very difficult. But we must also say that the motivation, faith and God's love for these people is the same as it has always been. We never stopped advancing in the midst of all that the Lord allowed us to go through.

Cry!

It doesn't take much to provoke tears in someone who has wept a lot. Crying brings consolation when you go through profound sadness. I say profound, for there is such a thing as pretended sadness, as well as tears of pretense. Some cry out of hate. Or because they feel impotent, when they cannot settle scores with those who have done them wrong, at least in their eyes. Some cry to get others to give them something, or to do something for them. And then there are those who cry hypocritically; or for business or gain; or to pressure others; or theatrically, to prove they are good actors. But I'm not interested in crying that is selfish or improperly motivated. I want to speak of those who really weep.

We should seek to rescue the treasure that is in the heart of someone who truly weeps. It's hard to describe what we perceive in tears. It is like something from deep within the person's being that leaks out as a moan. It's like the heart is breaking through the tears. It's as if, suddenly, a person who is unable to suffer any more, wants to be swallowed up by the earth as he cries. Or like the eyes of someone who is suffering but refuses to continue looking and tries to reject in some way the evil that he has seen. Like returning the sadness that has hurt him, in the form of salty drops of water.

People are like the sky. The sky releases its storm with rain. Only after the rain is calm restored and things return to normal. So it is also that a person who is meek and confident alleviates his storm within by weeping or raining, if we are able to say it that way, in order to better understand the situation.

People who are accustomed to live running from God never reveal their true self. Their nature is to speculate, and no one except God really knows them. Except when they weep, they loosen up and let something of value flow from within their mysterious and passionate being. If you see a person weeping, stand by his side in silence. Don't try to silence him unless God tells you to do so. You will surely not leave his side with empty hands. Let him weep, for when he releases from within what has to come out, you will discover how much he has inside, and how valuable it is.

Life is full of storms and reasons to weep. But a person's eyes are prepared to weep and cry. There is no storm that a person cannot overcome when his heart is yielded to God. As long as a person has his anchor fixed in God, there is no pain that can destroy him; God shows him how to gain something each time he weeps. It's like the psalmist who said: "He who goes out weeping, carrying seed to sow, will return with songs of joy, carrying sheaves with him" (Psalm 126:6).

19.
Time for the big trials

n fact the aforementioned times of trial did arrive! The ones that we hardly understood how they could be, nor how long they would last, although we always expected they would come. The worst part is that they caught us unawares. Brothers who made a bad business deal, whom we had to help get out of the mess; workers that made bad personal decisions that gradually affected the entire congregation; a valuable handmaiden like Sarah, responsible for the treasury, who left to go with the Lord, sinking most of us in profound sadness. And an endless number of problems that are too wearying to tell. Those things began to generate in us pressures, weeping and difficulties, that brought with them, still bring and will yet bring, a very steep cost. The trials shook our whole structure which was just coming together, and many of the less stable fell to the side of the road, with no strength left. The pain still clouds our vision with tears, not so much for those who went to be forever with the Lord, but for those who gave ground to bitterness, lack of faith in the work and division. They are the ones who run the greatest risk. Lord, forgive them and help them! In such circumstances, that's all we can say.

I am always awaiting the reencounter; every morning I ask God to let me see the return of those who left. With every year that passes, I hope to replace the pain in their hearts with a warm brotherly embrace, and show them that while they were away and saddened, we have not lowered our arms, but rather have done everything possible so that the anticipated and longed-for reunion might be really joyful, and bear much fruit.

If you want to reach your destination

When heavy fog is present, only those who know the region well can perceive the pathway. In such conditions, seeing includes the sum of what the eyes can perceive, what is remembered, and the care taken by the one who is walking.

When you live in the countryside, such things are learned quite well, for they are frequently experienced. When you have to put up with them, they are distasteful, but once experienced, they become precious wisdom that never loses its value. Of course for someone who is thankful, things will always work out better. For when you live with gratitude the experiences that come your way, you take advantage of everything that happens.

God gives wisdom to the simple. When you draw near to him, like the person who finds refuge after much searching, you will learn at his side. God owns everything, he is generous by nature and, besides, he rewards those who love him. And it is well known that, among those who know him, his attributes are evident in all he does. For that reason, the believer is different from other persons, no matter how wise they are. The person who believes in God wants to be at his side, and when you stay at his side a while, you will surely learn to live and to triumph. The truth is that even when you are a believer for many years, and have a lot of faith, or you serve God with all your heart, you can still have bad days. Days in which, unexpectedly, everything seems covered with a dense fog that makes it hard to see where you are walking.

So you have to confide in your eyes as you walk along the pathways, whether these are known or unknown. Perhaps you have never stopped to think about it, but you know how to follow the tracks. And your eyes, after observing so many paths, are accustomed to them. And even when the pathway you are now walking is strange to you, you should remember that once you know one pathway, you know the basics of all of them. And when your eyes are unable to see because of the fog, confide in your memory, so you won't have to stop walking. Your memories are nothing else but valuable maps that help you to find the treasures that life hides near the pathways. And when it's hard to see and your memory also tends to fade due to the fog, take hold of the wisdom that you have achieved; it will make you wise to take each step; and if you walk carefully, you will not likely stumble. Of course, do not forget God who made the pathways, grants the memories and imparts wisdom; he is always happy to do what we cannot do. Even when he doesn't walk with us, he sheds light on the pathway. He cannot make us remember what we have not lived, but he allows us to see that memory always precedes hope. He is faithful and never leads us to walk in a place for which he has not formerly taught us that which is indispensable for us to reach our destination. He will not take the precautions that are our responsibility, but he will affirm the rock onto which we step, if it happens to be loose.

Nothing is nicer than to move forward; when you advance, you feel that you are still alive; and being alive is all that is required for God to do wonders in your life.

20.
Sarah

S he repeated Psalm 23 until her voice completely faded away. She seemed to continue saying it, as her lips moved without a sound. Trying to help, we continued repeating it near her ear. That was our last goodbye, the last breath of Sarah's life full of psalms. She started slowly fading away, very quietly, without a whimper, just as she had always lived. Her mother was at her bedside and I on the opposite side; the way the three of us had agreed it should be if she left us; just as we had always wanted.

There in our poor neighborhood of tin houses and dirt floors, remained her "little ones," with their broken sandals and soiled faces, waiting for her, not understanding what had happened. The hard life on the street that is their lot gives them little time to stop for another pain; they know that life goes on and if they are detained, it's harder to catch up later.

Sarah was a worker for the Lord. One of the best. With a simplicity and humility seldom seen. And with an unquenchable faith in the love of her whole life, the Lord Jesus, in whom she trusted with the faith of a child. Every day she prayed that we might have the money to pay the bills and buy food for everyone and, of course, every day we received what was needed. Still in the office is her low white desk, with brown doors and convenient drawers, where she kept all she used to serve the God she always loved; the same one that she hurried away to meet forever.

The earth covered her remains in the poor section of the cemetery, under a large tree where she will always be remembered. When her birthday came around, the first she would ever miss, we placed a picture with her testimony on her tomb as a gift. And a little house, simple like herself, so that the sad friends who passed by could tear off a sheet that tells of her life and of Jesus. Many hundreds of sheets have been carried away so far, and some have called our home to tell of their need and ask for help. She continues to proclaim Jesus through those pages. And she continues to say that all things work together for good to those who love God, for there is a purpose in everything.

For an absent daughter

Who said that anything can be purchased with money? Who said that everything passes away? Who said that everything will be forgotten? If I had the money I would try. I would purchase from God even a few minutes with her. I would give everything I have for just a few minutes, and I would do so with joy. Today is her mother's birthday and I don't know what to give her to make her happy. The days pass, and her soul needs consolation again; yesterday's is not enough. Yesterday's argument won't help us today. It seems harder and harder to find reasons to continue. It's because we miss the one who is gone forever; it's the way life is when we are far from someone we have loved so much.

But we can't continue to think on such things. We need to say this; it's better to speak than to implode with sadness. Or at least write it down. When I write, no one is obliged to listen; only those who are interested will read it. You can even read a little and then take a break. Everyone is too sad to listen to the burden I carry.

I seek among my possessions something by which to remember her, something she has written, or some forgotten keepsake. It occurs to me that maybe before she left for good, she went through my things to leave some hidden message; crumbs that might serve to lift me for the road ahead; sparks to help keep my faith afire to the end. But I find nothing new. Listen to her recorded voice, read what she wrote, gaze at her photo, remember some anecdote, is hardly sufficient. I am nothing special, just one more person; someone that lost part of what he most loved, and has not found a way to live without it.

But it won't always be this way! All that hope sowed in the fertile soil of the soul will bear its fruit; we must wait a while, but the fruit will appear. All that faith awaits will come; without a doubt it will come. Faith does not admit failures; even when victories are not anticipated, they will come; even if heaven did not exist, it would call it into existence; even if there were no consolation, it would be found... or created. So much love cannot be for nothing; so much hope cannot remain without results; so much desire to see her will not be in vain. No, Lord!

21.
Run for your life!

" The boat is sinking! The work is lost!" some shouted. And it really looked like that was the case. We all came under a collective psychosis. Someone sounded the false alarm: We've got to get out of here! And we all got scared. Many left, causing us to face another exodus. Others remained, but doubting, not sure whether they had made the right decision. And the rest, although we felt sure we had done the right thing, began to think it would be impossible to save everything.

That situation greatly affected the work. It overburdened the workers, since they had to cover an additional post beside their own. It produced an economic chaos. And the meetings to clarify matters and encourage those that remained became our daily task.

We were jumping around and running for a while, and some even had the sensation that we would get sick and be unable to survive. Threatening telephone calls, false prophecies that instilled fear, the strangest temptations, the most complicated doubts, the most unexpected disobediences, and the ease with which some abandoned their post, were daily occurrences. Every time the telephone rang or someone called at the door, we trembled, anticipating the worst. Those were difficult days, in which everything turned sour.

Some of those who at the outset had promised everlasting love for God and commitment to this vision to serve among the needy, were the first to leave, after having given place to complaints and criticism. This surprised us and was very hard to understand, since we did not expect such from dearly beloved colleagues. Only the Lord knows the truth, and he will be merciful and he is the one who forgives. But even though everyone was hurt, those of us who remained did not slack. Baptisms, meetings, teaching, home groups, new crops and harvests and the children's meetings continued in spite of it all. And today we can still say: Ichabod: Until now the Lord has helped us!

Remedy for complaints

The beauty was breathtaking! It happened suddenly. As he walked he had to avoid thorns and rocks in that narrow path made by goats and other animals. He had come a great distance; he had even lost his way. And now his steps were much slower, while swallowed up in his thoughts and his problems. He was very tired; it was getting late and there was probably still a long way to go. The steep hill before him was quite pronounced and difficult; perhaps it was because he was weary, but it seemed like the steepest he had climbed all day. He was not that surprised, for those who walk in the mountains know that it always seems the same; you often have the sensation that the hill you are climbing is the highest. And when you get to the top, you discover that it was the smallest of all that yet need to be climbed. In such a situation, you almost wish you hadn't been born.

Then suddenly, everything changed. The unexpected occurred! The hill he just climbed was not just one more mountain: it was the last one. Now, stretched out before his surprised gaze was the most wonderful valley he had ever seen. The mountain that he had just finished climbing on that rough and rugged path, from the other side, appeared as a lovely fertile meadow that looked completely different. In the midst of a brilliant green, in a great valley in the distance, could be seen a group of houses with red roofs, surrounded by tall trees. A winding brown path moved out from the small village and disappeared at the other end of the valley, where the mountains continued.

It took a while to recover from the surprise, and then he began to feel bad. He felt he had no right to complain throughout most of the day. No right at all! He felt miserable, and was unable to keep walking. He sat down on a rock, unable to stop gazing even an instant on that amazing scene laid out by God's own hand. The whole scene worked its way into his soul with message and everything. He heard not a word, but what he saw spoke clearly to his heart that from that day his life would change forever.

It's impossible to remain stubborn before God's majestic greatness! He really loves us. Even while we are pondering vanities, God only seeks our good. We tremble before our problems, but God is preparing for us triumphs that will make history. While we complain about what has been dealt to us in life, God is waiting to see all that the trials will produce in us.

Before we complain about having to walk over ground that has been plowed, let us look carefully, because it just might be that God is setting up a garden for us. Before complaining about the persons close to us, we should be careful; perhaps God has placed them there to shape our life, so that we can learn at their side what is missing in order to fulfill our dreams.

What do you do when something like this happens?

22.
Adulam grows

A new farm. A new children's group. More work, more expenses, more problems. Yet, at the same time, more brothers and sisters and more blessings. Willingness to pay a high price is the only way the work can grow. Faith needs an open field to work, and we needed to do something to keep the failure from crushing us. We decided to present some new projects before the Lord and he answered our prayers. The small economic efforts that until that moment had been effective gave place to others, much better, in order to face the new demands. And, as had always been the case, the Lord was faithful. God gave us new places to sell our merchandise, workshops and better businesses.

Being as careful as possible, and with prayer, we began to build up the team of workers. We held lengthy meetings to learn everything we could in the shortest time possible. This was often quite tiring. But little by little a good group of workers emerged who, in spite of their youth and lack of experience, were able to manage things well. Every day we worked to keep a team spirit, the importance of which we learned by studying each detail and putting into practice what we learned time and again.

Some days were very difficult, since the new projects required all our effort. Both the brothers themselves and the administration required our special attention. Again, God was faithful and helped us so that, one by one, our plans were fulfilled. Every time we look at the farms, or consider the bills that have been paid, or the legal processes, or the new believers, we praise God for having guided us in all this work.

With every day that passes a sequel appears of the old problems we had to face which, in the final analysis, are not very different from those indicated in God's word and which always seek to impede God's great work. Nor are they very different from those faced by any other brother. But even when the pathway has obstructions and problems, God never lacks resources to overcome them. So we seek to live every day in the midst of that reality: always trusting God's good hand to guide us wherever we should go.

Prisoners of hope

The Bible tells us that God will give us new names. Every one of his children will receive a new name. What a wonder! The Lord's tenderness is immeasurable; that becomes very clear when he speaks to us about himself, when he tells us something about ourselves, and when he makes plans for our benefit. His promises are unique. In Zechariah 9:12, in an amazing expression of his dominion, love, tenderness and consolation, God opens his mouth and prophesies over his people with singular clarity, like the brightest mornings from childhood in my village. Just as simply, as if in passing, or declaring an obvious fact, with absolute assurance, without a sign of a doubt, with no possibility of misinterpretation, leaving us breathless and speechless, he says, among other things: "Return to the stronghold, you prisoners of hope. Even today I declare that I will restore double to you" (NKJV). That fascinates me! From this day forward I would like for that to be my name: Omar, prisoner of hope. What a beautiful word! It fills my soul with unspeakable joy; my spirit leaps within me; and my hand grabs the paper avidly, scratching out the words as fast as I can, trying to not lose a single thought. Prisoner of hope!

"Prisoner" has reference to a jail. And that implies the inability to leave, that someone is watching, your will has been restricted, you cannot travel or even take a walk, limited personal decisions, being in a strange place, locked up and without knowing how things will turn out, or when conditions will change.

"Hope" means expecting something good, for hope always refers to something pleasant. I never hope for something bad. If someone is expecting the worst, you cannot say that he has hope. Because hope means that the present situation is not important, that I accept what I am, for my vision and my life are focused on my hope. My anxiety has been calmed down by my hope, for hope has no anxiety (there is anxiety when hope is absent). It implies meekness, patience in trials, lessons learned, wrinkles on the face worn with dignity. No hurry, assurance written with letters of fire in the soul, and a readiness to share that emotion with others. It enables me to speak all day about the same thing; and to keep silent before the aggressor, for my heart is not focused on what I am now living, but on what I hope for.

The preposition "of" refers to belonging, dependence, recognition of an owner. Existence for something. It is to be under control, in the best sense, because it is accepted voluntarily. Prisoner of hope! I am a captive of hope.

One day God sought me; he spoke clearly to me, in a way I could understand. And I determined to stay with him forever. I will be a pilgrim on earth, following his steps; and I will hope for what he promised, regardless of how long it takes, for I know that one day I will enjoy that which was promised. I am a prisoner from the moment in which, by my own choice, I stepped into his prison and decided to be his captive. And I will be a prisoner until I die, for he is God; who can escape from his prison? Moreover, who would want to escape once he knows him? What delightful foolishness!

When I was not yet a believer I wrote the following, without really understanding it:

I expected to find hope,
the expectation of hoping with joy,
that someone might bring me hope,
and help me to make changes in my life.

And expecting to have that hope,
with expectation I hoped every day.
And after waiting so long it seemed that,
little by little, hope was lost.

But then one day the best destroyer of sad poetry that I have known came into my life and he inspired me to write other lines:

But that hope, one day,
became real hope.
Jesus came, and brought hope,
the hope of living with him for eternity.

23.
Red Alert! Workers needed

With many of the disciples of the early leaders, those that were won to the Lord at the beginning, we were unable to develop properly and they were not especially effective as servants of the Lord. They got left aside by the work of the older ones, and by our own failure to delegate responsibilities. Today most of them are faithful believers, with stable families, although, generally speaking, with little knowledge in practical matters, slow to occupy important positions, and reluctant to make significant decisions.

We need workers! The lack of workers implies chaos for a work like this. Workers needed is an expression that brings us pain, and a constant crying out to God. It refers to a hoped-for solution, but also impossible to achieve without the Lord's help. Workers are needed! Who will occupy these positions? Another one left us! And now, what will we do? Phrases and questions like this are frequently heard among us. And that burden becomes a prayer every day: Lord, send workers to help in your vineyard!

The work continues today. There are still struggles, still tears and still weariness. Someone who is disposed to give up discovers a thousand reasons to get discouraged; but the one who continues to be faithful to God perceives the miracle of his care and blessing. He observes the way in which the Lord's protecting and generous hand is upon us and upon all that we are doing in faith. The daily task is accomplished, even with insufficient workers. Those who have recently begun to work obtain a practical knowledge of God that they would not otherwise acquire.

God is good, and when accidents occur, he always gives us another opportunity to remedy what is irremediable. And in these times, bit by bit, many dear brothers move forward toward their place in God's work.

We are always waiting for God's action, his mercy and his saving and restoring love for people. We await his provision of new workers, filled with the Spirit. Every day our eyes turn toward his hands with faith and hope, just as the sentinel awaits the morning light, just as the servant looks to the hand of his master. We know that the Lord of the harvest will provide the workers that are needed.

Wet ears

They have wounded you, they have ruined and robbed you, they have humiliated and challenged you. Just as we said when we were children: "They have left your ears wet." And instead of facing your opponent, you cry in a corner out of impotence, while your enemies are enjoying what is rightfully yours. How shameful! What a great shame for one who confessed faith in Christ. What a paradox! You thought you would be the victor but others have taken away what was yours. Psalm 23 cannot have the facts backward; you are the one who sits at the prepared table, not your enemies. If you don't quickly reverse this idea within you, what will you say to the Lord when you give account of yourself? Can you explain to me what you will tell him?

You dare not wait a minute longer! You must assume again the right attitude. You must go before God, cry before him, confess your failure, and wait there a while on your face in his presence, so that through his Spirit he might instruct you about what you should do to come out on the other side and save this situation. Don't do anything before you talk with God. Don't come to terms with the enemy. Don't give up any ground; he may rob you, but don't give up anything willingly. Because what you give up, you turn over to him and then you have no right to claim it later. On the other hand, if he robs you, that is different, for concerning that which has been stolen God says that he will do something special. He says that he will return to his children, in his time, all that the enemy stole from them.

Trust in this truth, go to God and get ready to see the result. God is true and faithful. He will not allow those who trust in him to suffer loss, confusion or shame. In his time he will give the victory to his children, and it will be total, unquestionable, broad, generous, brilliant, inspiring, poetic, beautiful, clear, holy and eternal. I have given my life for this truth and I will believe it until I die; it has never failed me and I know it will never fail. My dream is that all come to know this truth and embrace it to their last breath. May the earth be filled with the knowledge of the Lord Jesus Christ! Amen.

24.
The youth

*Y*oung people are one of God's great resources for this kind of service, due to their almost indomitable enthusiasm, their great desire to please God once they know him, their great strength, and the beauty of their soul. They transform chaos into normalcy in a short time. Of course you need to know how to work with them. If you expect punctuality, you won't always achieve it; but once they apply their hands to the task each day, they won't stop until quite late.

We only needed to wait for them to catch the desire to work and then we made giant steps. We had to be careful that their enthusiasm didn't catch us without plans. If the plans were in place, then they produced significant and positive advances. Of course, wherever there are young people, you are surely going to have a lot of excitement!

Many of them, with very little experience or knowledge and without the assurance that comes with years, serve God with their whole heart. They sleep when they can, eat at any hour, are willing to sacrifice themselves and give everything. Thank God for the youth! When they are near, everything is different: they weep, they fail, they talk, they laugh and triumph, all with intensity. All the dimensions are excessive; the messes are bigger, but the triumphs as well. And although at times it is painful to see them fail, they win for God places, persons and resources that hardly anyone else can achieve. Anyone who has a good bunch of young people is rich indeed, I can assure you. For a good reason the Lord pointed out:

"Blessed is the man who has his quiver full of them," referring to children.

The young people here are valuable boys and girls that, even with their ups and downs, their hurts, dropouts and vices, once transformed by the Lord, constitute a constant renewal in the life of those of us who are older in our service to God.

God didn't make the church up only of youth, but he gave them a place and they are incomparable. A church without young people is poor, because a significant part is missing. It would be equally limited if there were no old folks or children. All are useful when we learn to function, as long as we don't seek the preeminence or look down on others. Young people provide strength to build the house that the adult designed, that the older person dreamed, that the wife longed to have, and the child needed. And God, as always, placed his seal on what pleases him, providing all that is necessary to build it. This is our experience with God and with the youth. On one hand we see the ever present supply and power of the creator and, on the other, the effective strength of that outcropping of creation that are young people.

Creation

Some day I should write a book, I thought; even if only one copy were printed. A book of several chapters, where each one tells the story of a different one of the persons around me. A book that makes known something of those mysterious human beings with whom I have lived and that seem to have been created by God at special times. Maybe some day when I am inspired or happy and desire to do some-

thing different. Something masterful and fresh. Something like a special essay. For even the flaw in each one seems to have been put there on purpose!

Almost all of them came out of the night; they come from the darkness, really dark, like you see in some of the suburbs, where most of the inhabitants have a similar characteristic: they are professional failures.

All have had long journeys and have witnessed the human drama from different points of view. Experience has made them wise. Personalities, you name it! Profoundly mysterious. Stubborn, due to the hunger they have known. Imaginative, by necessity. Thankful, due to so many desires for things that were delayed or denied. Loving, for so much seeking of kindness. Like Gabriel, the skinny guy, pure gold; like Jorge, who died while seeking a fantasy; like Gloria, whom God rewarded with heaven; like Mayito, the silent one, who wanted to live; like the Jew, who started farms; like Sara, and like so many other unforgettable characters already with the Lord; and the many that are still seeking their new name.

I could never be the same after meeting them. They helped me greatly when I had to teach my children to be servants of God and to live and die for the Lord. For that reason I am forever thankful, and I owe them homage.

To be able to write about them fills my soul with gratitude and desire to praise God, for God, in his genial way, with richness and good taste, has surrounded himself with these people. And from his perspective he sees them all together, and always enjoys their company and their crazy notions. How I would like to always live that way!

I love them sincerely, and they know that. At times I came to think that some, to keep me from forgetting them or ceasing to love them, died before myself, some even in their youth. They lived their life rapidly, as if fearing they might fail, and then left for good, leaving only an indelible memory.

For all that I have said I encourage you to not bother the Lord asking him about whatever seems to be unjust or difficult. He is working in your life and will make it beautiful. Your life will be part of something wonderful that at this point, no matter how hard you try, you cannot possibly imagine. Don't interrupt the creator, just wait on him and obey. He will do all that is needed to assure you of success in the end. Don't forget that you are a combat soldier, and from your point in the conflict you cannot see the whole panorama, so it is better to be obedient to the one who sees it all.

25.
There is hope!

*Y*et there is hope! And when there is, hardly anything else matters. Each day it seems to us that we won't make it to the end. We live with the sensation that our health won't hold out; at times it seems like the pain and the work are overwhelming, but every day ends in blessing, just as it should be with God's children. We work until we cannot do any more, and even when it seems like it's not enough, little by little we see a great advance in the Lord's work. It's all difficult and at times very slow, due to the lack of experience and resources. But today the dark tunnel in which we walk has a bright spot in the middle, and it doesn't look like it's a train coming from the other end! For if that were the case, its brightness and size would rapidly increase. Instead, we can clearly see that it is growing as we move forward. Glory to God!

Sometimes I think that we should be in better condition than our present reality. It occurs to us that we should require more from the others. It also seems that many presume that we cannot fail or make a mistake. But it only appears to us that way, maybe because our life is open to the gaze of everyone, all day long. We call upon many and we go wherever it is needed in search of God's blessing. Maybe that is what brings on so much criticism and the diverse opinions, which we recognize are sometimes discouraging to many. There are mornings when, amazingly, almost everyone seems to be in the dumps. In those circumstances we hardly know how to proceed. But our good God comes to our aid, and things soon return to normal. We learn that behind every great struggle there is hidden God's great blessing; and once encouraged again, we jump forward to catch the blessing that we so need to continue. Thus, like the boy in the Bible, every day we place our bread and fish in the Lord's hands, expecting him to multiply them.

We have time, since our purpose is not to demonstrate anything to anyone, but just to be like the Lord desires and reach heaven like the rest. We don't need to hurry to achieve some earthly goal.

There is hope! And time. God is with us and there are young workers nearby.

Another reality!

In the middle of the surprise is where we need to be. There where the hardest battles are fought; where heaven, showing its authority, rescues men from hell; where death is our uninvited companion, and even the strong weeps in wonder. That is where we must be, if we mean to win something that has real value. If the enemy competes with men, he has the advantage; of that we are sure. And he knows that. He has vast experience, and he is always there wanting to take control. He sees at a distance the strong and useful ones, deceives them when he can and winds up dominating them. For that reason the church must rescue those people from hell, if it really loves them.

I know a little bit about such matters. And the results that I have obtained are considerably less than I have been able to learn; but I have clearly seen the reality. I know quite well that someone who moves into that arena cannot expect others to toss him bouquets. It is not easy to come out victorious in every incursion that we carry out, but once we have fought in that arena, there is no desire to fight in another, for it is like moving backwards.

That is where the best people act, move, suffer and work. Those that could become the most noble, faithful and useful, if they had not been overtaken by a despotic and cruel enemy, that always wants to dominate them. Whatever we can rescue from those circumstances will surely turn out to be the best.

Our nothing turns out to be much for a God that is so good, to whom we owe so much. Perhaps it is very little that we have been able to accomplish, but even though it seems like little, we can offer him something when we come before his throne. We will offer to him what we have achieved, whatever we have been able to save in our times of struggling.

Some day I will make that round! The one that I have so often imagined in my better dreams. Some day I'll be able to see it all together, all that we were able to accomplish each time that God helped us to overcome that false "common sense", that which always limits us, so as to get into the arena and rescue those fiery coals. I am sure I will have that opportunity. God said so. And if he said so, it will happen. That day I will let my soul express the best that I have kept inside. And everyone will know how much I have loved God and his work, how much I have loved the brothers and the lost. Of course they will also know how limited I am. And how many defects I really have. But that too will constitute the spoils of war placed in the Lord's hands, because for someone who is strong it is easy to fight against ferocious enemies. But a victory obtained by the weak is worth more than that of the strong!

26.
Honesty in giving and giving ourselves

❝ If you receive something for a grinding wheel, don't use it to eat. If you receive money for rice, don't buy shoes." I always thought in those terms. That's the way I have lived and taught my children and the disciples. Honesty should be quite simple. When people don't do things this way, they get into problems. People that give for a certain purpose want to see their desires realized. If we don't fulfill what they have indicated, they will not give again. I learned that secret in the streets, even though there you couldn't live that way. But when I turned to God, I came to see that he thinks and acts that way, and it helps those of us who trust in him to live the same way. The Lord wants to bless and prosper the honest and faithful steward that takes care of that which has been entrusted to him. Someone who doesn't handle things properly should not expect to be blessed. In this kind of work you must not apply the popular saying: The end justifies the means. Not so, Lord!

Medicine, doctors, teachers, vehicles, food and everything needed to carry out this kind of work are expensive and difficult to obtain; and as the group grows, the demand for everything also grows. But God has warehouses full of elements that we need, and he is ready to give them in abundance. We only need to learn to ask in faith and wait on him!

I should not ask for donations just to increase my own capital, but to do something significant for others. There is no better way than this to learn the great truth declared by the Lord Jesus: "Seek and you will find." It goes without saying that he who gives to the poor is always benefitted personally, without having to touch a cent of that which doesn't belong to him. God has enough for everyone and blesses our work. And he causes us to prosper more than we could imagine!

Chickens and generosity

When you have money, four chickens is nothing; but when you don't have anything, four chickens are a real treasure.

He is a poor boy, whose only capital in life is four chickens. A few days ago, one of them laid an egg; something that he took care of very well, since it was the only thing of real worth that he had received in a long time. When others asked him, he simply responded: "We mustn't eat it, we must wait."

But for a birthday you can't go without a gift, even if you have been invited. You should always take something; even if the one celebrating the birthday is a little girl. She may receive many gifts from her family and is unaware of the lack from others; but it's better to take something. Whenever we have doubts, it is always more economical to decide in favor of what is easy; and the easiest option is to take nothing.

In the celebration there are many nice things to eat. There are games and a lot of laughs; and an abundance of those delightful sounds that children make when they are happy. There are many children to play and when they do, the hours fly past. Soon it's time to return home. It's a shame, but we have to go home. We must greet the family and not forget to say thanks for the invitation.

But what should you do when it's time to say goodbye to the one whose birthday is being celebrated, and you find her deep in thought, sad and seated in a corner? What should you do if you discover when you ask, that the sadness is due to a lack of gifts? Not much, if she was expecting something more, something that the invited children would bring. There is only one thing to do: get a gift. And when it comes to giving, we should give the best. That's what they say, and it is what we were taught. Besides, it's what Jesus would do.

A newspaper for wrapping and a used bag is enough. When you are a child, the values are different. Life is more simple. A newspaper, a simple bag, a single egg and the miracle takes place. The child celebrating is happy; her parents weep when they observe the attitude of the generous visitor. The mother of the little boy sees the fruit of what she taught him; a pastor, interested in anecdotes, finds a new motive to write. God now has a new tool to propagate his message; and some — who can know when, where and how? — discover through this account their way back to God… or they learn to be generous… or it will make them a little kinder. Who says the poor have nothing to give!

27.
Love until it hurts

V ery few people are willing to renounce everything in order to seriously cooperate for the extension of the kingdom of God. And fewer still are ready to do so among the people who are most needy. Unfortunately, many see in the gospel an opportunity to advance and achieve goals that they could otherwise never reach. We have only one life, and we can choose to live it intensely for ourselves, or dedicate the greater part of it to serve God and others. Often our life is spent in the search for personal objectives, dreams filled with humanity and goals that God would never own. This reality saddens me, for it simply means, as I understand it, that such lives are built on sand; and at the end of the road is total chaos. Let's not forget that Jesus said that he who saves his life will lose it, but that the one who gives his life for others, will win.

May God grant another opportunity to those that have dropped out along the way! May God help us to reach the end in victory! Sometimes the life that we have to live in this kind of work means that even the strongest would prefer to live another way. At times, some opinions make us feel like we have chosen the worst option; or that we have deceived ourselves. There are times when we feel that we will never get through this experience without getting hurt. And if we pay attention to what they tell us, some will have second thoughts, trapped in those real spider webs of endless words, emitted without meaning.

But we are still here, in spite of it all. Persisting stubbornly, as one countryman said to me, "like cat whiskers." Without lowering our arms, without measuring our efforts, without ceasing to love, without losing faith, embracing hope like a child embracing her mother when afraid. Praying at every opportunity, so that nothing happens "by chance," so that everything happens under God's oversight. For if we don't have his approval, it's all in vain.

Until it hurts! Until the end, as the Lord said, we have to persevere without questioning, without murmuring, without giving up, with our eyes on the recompense: our arms full of poor people that are able to reach heaven!

Verses to scatter along the way

If you sing, sing out so the poor person can understand you; he is poor, and for that reason he has no material treasures nor refined tastes. He only has worries that he has acquired at a great price. And wisdom learned in the places where he has walked; and that is not the same as the other kind of wisdom. The other is learned in class rooms, and sometimes by obligation; but this wisdom can only be learned by living. When you live, you use up time, and time is like a hammer that records experiences in your soul bruskly but unforgettably. That's why we have to sing out clearly and sensibly, so that the poor person perceives that he is understood, and while he listens, he rejoices to learn that his suffering was not in vain, since someone else understands it.

If you laugh, laugh out loud so that no one is offended and everyone can share your laugh, for joy is hard to come by and nothing is more welcome. Very few will cast laughter out of their house without listening to it; everyone will reserve for it the best place so that it will stay with them; although sometimes they are unsuccessful. Be generous with your laughter; it won't cost you much, and for the one who laughs with you you will be a hero that has come just in time.

If you weep, weep out loud, for otherwise no one will hear you, and therefore no one will console you. Everyone is tired of hearing complaints, since most of us complain all the time. Weep for something worthwhile; weep without fear and without desperation, for real weeping improves your heart and makes you more sensitive. Let everyone know why you are weeping; many may leave when they don't know what to say or they don't want to share your burden, but someone will stay by your side. And because he will interpret the sincerity of your weeping, he will console you and you will be better afterward.

If you love, love openly, since love costs everything; and it's not wise to waste something worthwhile on nothing. Love whoever you will, without requiring anything in exchange; risk the adventure of living always to give of yourself. And when the bearers of oppression and fear of not knowing how to love come to mock you because you love freely without requiring anything, laugh at them, in secret, and leave them alone; for those who don't love that way, without expecting gratitude, know nothing worth listening to.

If you believe, believe openly, believe truly; believe in God alone, because all else cannot be trusted. Believe him like a child, for only by believing that way will you be able sometime to sing, laugh, weep and love truly and openly. These four things are all implicit in that phrase of Jesus, so well known and fearsome: "Without me, you can do nothing."

28.
Jesus, the street

For the peace and encouragement of all, God spoke one day and revealed to us that "Jesus is the only way to the Father." A "way" is a street; and the street is the place where most of us have been raised. A well known and familiar place for the poor and those who live on the margin; a space that provides everything you need to live, if in fact you understand its reality and its codes. Jesus said to us: "I am your street, your new street;" and that greatly encouraged us, for then we could help the young people understand Jesus' proposal in a language familiar to them. If Jesus is the street, we can understand that in him we find everything we need: friends, truth, pastimes, security, language, customs, home, shelter, food, adventure, love, peace, liberty, all that is novel and attractive. Everything that we need to live. "I can do all things in Christ, my street." Then we won't need a supplementary truth, nor alternatives, nor extraordinary revelations; he is enough.

In this simple way the young people could understand God's will, expressed in his message to the world. God has a purpose for us, and it is based on his kingdom, in the lordship of Christ, and on the group of truths that we need to understand to live the new life that God provides. Many young people are willing to give everything if they can have Jesus, the pearl of great price. Jesus is the most popular person among those who have left the darkness with a desire to'change their life, for they feel that they are understood and cared for by him.

I pray to God that we will never tire of teaching all that we have learned, for without understanding you can't go very far, even if there is a street. It was half understood truths, half believed, or half-lived, that led these people to failure; we must not allow them to repeat the experience. We have to teach them the truth, regardless of the cost.

The lonely ones that wait

Seated on the curb, with his gaze lost on the hot cement of the street, he holds his head with both hands. I understand the many thoughts that flash through his mind, driving him crazy. I know that he is suffering, that he can take no more, that he doesn't know where to go.

A driver who wants to park his car just where he is seated, honks the horn but is unable to get his attention. He insists over and over, until he finally gives up and parks somewhere else, as he curses.

He is a stranger with dirty clothes and broken shoes; a professional of pain and ignorance; an accident from a night of passion, that someone left on the street. No one would give two cents for his life; but he feels that he owns the sidewalk, the street. He was born there, and never knew another home. Life is hard to understand: some have everything, others have nothing, but everyone pays the same price. Today he received the worst news of his life: his street is not his. They have told him and shown him that his street is not his, and he must leave. How can he live with nothing of his own?

I knew that something had happened to him, for he is never alone and yet for a long time I have seen no one else with him. He has spent hours seated there, in the same position, as if he were asleep or dead. I should dare to look more closely at him; I should try to save him from his unknown pain; I should take advantage of this moment of confusion in his life. Maybe he will listen to me, maybe today he will listen to my well-used message of a village preacher.

The fear of failing and of being rejected is sometimes stronger than the love that I feel for people like him. What a shame! If he would listen to me, I could teach him to live with few things of his own, just as I do; I could tell him that for many years Christ has been everything for me. I could sit down next to him and share his frustration; I could explain to him about heaven that awaits those who believe in God as I do. But I have more vices that he; different kinds of vices, but vices, after all. I have the vice of common sense, religion, fears, of what I can do and what I can't do.

When will the day come when I stop acting as if heaven were mine! When will I be able to stop living as if the truth I learned from God were only for me! When will I really be able to do something for those who wait on the curbs of the street!

29.
We can too

God has always used common people to extend his kingdom! We are happy that we learned this simple but great truth. Certainly we have suffered many hurts, but by his grace this blessing has remained: "We too can serve God."

God doesn't need anyone to help him completely transform a person who humbles himself and places himself in his hands; but he prefers that his children help. God is able to do his job so well that those who know the person in question, following his transformation, can hardly believe the results achieved. And we are able to cooperate with that task. We just need to place ourselves unconditionally in his hands and obey his word. It's not enough to just understand it and talk about it to everyone; we need to live it. We need to think, speak and live in the same way, so that the world can know and believe what God can do. Otherwise they will think that what we have is simply another offer among all those that they hear every day.

If we are selling cheap stuff, if we have hidden agendas, in the end the world will know, for that is what many have done for centuries. But if the way we live is coherent, we will witness God moving as we desire.

The fact is that we too can serve God, we can do his will, for he does not despise the contrite heart that comes to him seeking shelter and wanting to live at his side. He will share his whole life.

We already understand that life is action, and God directs his action well and guides that of his children well.

Grass that hides heaven

"Tomorrow I'm not going with the team to work," my son firmly told me. Then he added: "The weeds have almost covered Mica's house. No one has gone to cut them, so I will do it."

"Fine," I responded. "Sounds good to me."

Mica, from the poor neighborhood. A little girl without a mother, without a family to care for her, seriously ill and almost without attention. She always has to have an oxigen tube connected. She lives in a dismantled shack that is so shameful that even the weeds try to cover it up. Today my son cut the grass, cleaned up the house, and chatted with her for a while. Mica was very happy with his visit and help… and then she died. She left for good! In a drastic way, just as her life had been.

What a loss! How difficult is this work! Never a day passes without something sad happening. But it all works together for good, for in the midst of the pain we discover the good character of a son. Like father, like son! Well done, he understood well. Now I can rest at ease! Elias inherited my perception to rescue people from hell and to be near them when they leave us to go to heaven. The neighborhood where we serve God is poor. A place of death, a place of violence, a place of pain. There are many sick because the whole place has been built over garbage. There is little food, no hospitals, no ambulances, no functioning telephones, not enough water, no social workers, no medicine. Nothing! Nothing good. Just pain. Hunger and pain. Misery and pain. Sadness and pain. Poverty and pain. Death and pain. Little faith… and pain and more pain. What can we do? Almost nothing. It's impossible to attend everyone; we're only able to calm the hunger once in a while; we have nothing to meet so much need. We can only pray that the word of God reach those children so they can believe and go to heaven, like Lazarus in the Bible.

People can only be saved through the foolishness of preaching. That is the truth! It's good doctrine. Today, when my children put it into practice, I understood that for those who are saved whom God wanted to call home, it's hard to leave if the weeds are high and the house is dirty. If we help them and clean their house, if we cut the weeds, they will be so happy that they will want to go and thank God personally that he remembered them through someone's help. Of course, when they see heaven, they don't want to return, even when the house is now nice and clean. That's a little painful for those of us who remain, for now there is someone else that we will miss.

But that's not so important! After all, that's our work!

30.
Our present reality

W e continue to do what we believe we should do. Each day we work, loving and advancing by faith. As long as there are poor people, we have to continue to feed them; as long as there are needy, we must continue helping them; as long as there are lost, we must continue to show them the way; and as long as there is strength, we continue in the struggle.

We pray that every meeting for the children might have their own place and the facilities that are needed. We struggle to help other ministries that began with us. We teach the best we can to all that have come to know Jesus among us. We continue to evangelize with hope and diligence. And we continue to work to improve all the properties that the Lord has given us, so that all of us can live a little better.

Our resources are better organized than before; and some of them that didn't bring in much profit and required a lot of effort, we stopped sustaining. With his great love the Lord has taught us new things through which we achieve better fruit with less effort. However, the greatest work continues to be done. We use every hour that we have to gather the fresh manna that God sends each day, and it's never lacking.

At times, the struggle wears out even the strongest of our "soldiers;" to the point that some have fallen along the way. But we help each other, and we wait for each other, so as to continue marching together. It goes without saying that, just as in the past, we face daily difficulties that at times seem humanly impossible to resolve; but God never lays a weight upon us that we are unable to bear. So that we humbly bear our burden, even though there are occasions when we complain a little. We all understand that the complaints are only because we don't want to carry the burden, not because we are unable to do so.

We are thankful and happy; we feel that we could not live any other way. We are always expecting the Lord to move, and when we perceive his slightest movement, we go there, waiting upon him, awaiting his signs, loving him and learning every day what he wants to teach us in his mercy.

We hope to continue this way, unless the Lord decides otherwise!

Please! Can you care for me?

It's the story of many: they live, desiring to be loved. They are willing to do anything to be accepted. They weep from so much waiting for an expression of appreciation or approval. Dreaming about being invited somewhere. Longing for an encounter or a return that never occurs. Life seems to escape them without any achievement. The long days pass and the hoped-for news never arrives. It's like the fable of the donkey with a carrot tied on a pole before him in order to get him to work. Walking, struggling, longing, desiring, believing what they say; and never reaching anything! This is the reality of many; a reality that makes a person cowardly, fearful, and drives him crazy.

Maria gets closer; a choked-off cry breaks up her voice; her eyes shine, about ready to break into tears. And a strange question dances on her lips: "Please, could you care for me?" If I answer no, I can avoid many problems, but I mess up many messages I have preached.

If I say Yes, I am coherent with what I believe, but I get involved in sinful problems that are not mine, loneliness, needs and… it's anybody's guess what else! Besides, I will have to go back to teaching the basics from the starting point. What is best? How should I respond? To make matters worse, I don't have much time to think because she is waiting for an answer this moment, and to delay more than necessary would make her think that the yes is really a no, or that the no is a yes. And her doubts will dismiss any good intention there may be. But it's not a matter to think about for long, I must be coherent. I have to keep saying Yes!

We must sell a bit more today: there is one more person at the table. Find another mattress, someone else is going to sleep in our home. We need to share what there is, keeping another person in mind. Or else, make the portions smaller. As Black always says: "We mustn't forget those whose luck has run out." When we have time, we need to review whether it's all right to accept the responsibility to care for someone who has asked for our love.

And the process repeats itself, and again we need to remind the one who is helping: If you see the person weep, don't ask him anything, just stand silently at his side; if she needs you, she will tell you why, or tell you something. If she asks you something, respond with love and concern. Don't injure her with your hopes nor with common phrases. If she tells you something, just listen in silence and with much attention; for she will speak softly and very little, as if it hurts her to do so, if she repeats what she already told you, it means double pain. If you want to, you can love her; but you must love her as she is, without ceasing to be herself.

How interesting… this matter of loving! True love really is a miracle! God tried everything with Job, without anyone being able to understand it, just to hear him say at the end: "My ears had heard of you, but now my eyes have seen you." After that phrase, the book is almost done. Hardly anything else needs to be said, once the lesson is learned. That's the reason we work as well! Just to see some day that someone else expresses his love to Jesus.

31.
What I think is coming

ven though I observe great weariness in the workers that occupy their places at the front, and a lack of polish and experience in those on the secondary line, I am very optimistic concerning what I believe God will do in our midst in the coming
years.

It is easy to find in our group serious flaws wherever you look.
We also recognize that, generally speaking, we would appreciate
greater collaboration from the brothers in the congregation that
are not one hundred per cent involved in this work. But we need
patience, for the lack of commitment of others may be due to the
lack of effectively communicating the vision. On the other hand, it
is certain that our habit of conforming and putting up with things
always threatens to dampen enthusiasm, and great projects are
often sacrificed on the altar of urgency; quality itself is sometimes
sacrificed. So much so that some abandon their posts gradually,
without calling attention to the fact. But it's also true that day to
day we are surprised by the Lord with the most wonderful and
unexpected miracles that anyone could imagine. We are also part
of the church; and the church is accustomed to going through terrible storms throughout the various stages of its history. It is not
the church that is in danger of ceasing to exist; it is ourselves, as
a group, that face such a danger. Individually, each one will find

himself at great risk if he doesn't react in time to obey. We need to do God's will! Even if it costs our life.

There are times when a phrase, spoken in different contexts, may have a variety of meanings. "God will do what he has to do" for some may be good news, while for others it could imply ruin. For some it can become a blessing, and for others, it may leave them outside God's plans. For some it could be cause for joy, while for others, great sadness and loss. For me, what God does makes more sense in the measure that I am able to participate in the matter. Every day it becomes more evident that we need to be transformed into protagonists and cease to be mere spectators, when it comes to living in the midst of events that, without a doubt, God is managing.

No one believes that governments and human power are in charge of determining our times. Or the chaotic end. Or the beginning of epochs of economic bonanza and the eradication of evil and violence. When people and governments act with arrogance, pretending to leave God aside while presenting poor and often used human ideas as if they were a universal panacea, the sentence of Jesus Christ is fulfilled, which he addressed to the Pharisees:

"Hypocrites, you clean the outside of the cup and dish, but inside they are full of greed and self-indulgence."

Only God can help us achieve the true change that everyone hopes for. Many may try to do it alone, but they will not succeed; even the one who has the best intention will fall in the pit of corruption and failure. But God will do wonders with his people. Without taking into account those who believe themselves powerful, and in spite of the magic they promise to perform, God will teach his own concerning the need to not evade reality, the importance of saving energy, funds and efforts. God alone will teach his people the truth concerning ecology, care of the planet and the proper and wise use of our natural resources. Every other system, no matter how good and transparent it seems, will become unavoidably corrupt. One doesn't need to be a prophet to predict it, for all of us know that while the mind thinks about how to implement a plan to benefit others, even the most humble sectors of the population, thousands of corrupt minds invent ways to take advantage of the plan to fill their pockets. But none who act against the poor will prosper, for they act against God himself.

In the midst of chaotic and sad situations, God continues to be God. He has already said: "Without me, you can do nothing." And he waits for some of us to believe that, no doubt, he will lead us to victory, to the knowledge of his will and to a glorious harvest of lives for his kingdom. It always shocks me to realize that an error, or a simple lack of patience to wait upon God, can turn me aside from the way and cause me to miss what he will do in these times to make himself known to multitudes. May the Lord grant me strength!

But in spite of everything, every day here there is news that tells of the arrival of another blessing; the work will increase to the point that we cannot finish it; and the needy will continue to arrive. Only God can know exactly what is coming; but we anticipate times of great harvest of persons seeking to know the love of God.

Finally, I want to say that up to this point it has been very good to work and experience God's truth in this way. To this day life has been exciting for me, since God's ever present help has become a real and surprising adventure. And if everything continues in a similar way, it will be quite interesting to live through what is coming. I am even encouraged to challenge each one of those reading this little story to accompany me to live out what the way before us promises. We will see you there!

A different ending

When the editing was concluded on this book I was told that the final part was not satisfactory, and that I should try something better. I did not know what to do, nor how to respond. I went home discouraged and I began writing the first thing that occurred to me, as if seeking a nice solution; if only to calm the unpleasant feeling produced by that counsel. I hoped that from the deepest part of my being God would inspire me with something really good. The following is what came into my mind at that moment.

If you could join night and day for once, what would be the result? Perhaps the first thing that comes to mind is that we would find ourselves before a gray day or a clear night. And it would be perceived by each spectator according to his own emotional state. But if we keep in mind that light is never joined to darkness, that may not be the result. Maybe there would be a little light in some places, such as we see in our home at night, or a little darkness during the day, such as when we leave our house darkened on a summer day to keep it a little cooler. Perhaps there would be a struggle between the night and the day, disputing the right to rule, and trying to impose the particular characteristics of one or the other. Maybe the nighttime fears would not be so frightful, for in some places there would be light; maybe the day's worries wouldn't be so bad, due to a little darkness here and there; it might bring more calm.

I think that is what happens with Jesus in the lower places where we live and serve God: Jesus is the day that came to fill with light the neighborhoods covered by the most persistent darkness. And for that reason, they now seem to be uncertain, mysterious, fearful, and at the same time, interesting. At times they seem terrible and occasionally they awaken the most unlikely compassion. At one point the most inhumane violence reigns, then suddenly you hear an accordion that some little fellow, with desires to be a preacher, is playing while *trying to guide children to the kingdom of God. Then you see drugs moving with a napkin around the neck, devouring precious young lives and suddenly a soldier of Jesus passes by, taking by the hand of someone he has won who, after a period of time winds up being a missionary. On another occasion, hunger cramps the stomach muscles and a little further along someone unaware of this, who fears nothing, is preparing a meal for many in a stained pot over a wood fire, and brazenly wearing a cap that says "LIFE", but he doesn't know it because it's written in another language.*

Jesus went into the neighborhood, and the neighborhood wasn't able to change its general aspect to welcome him; that's why it looks this way. That's why the streets are dirty and the faces of its inhabitants haven't been washed. That's why a party wasn't planned. He came without anticipation and took them all by surprise. If they had known he was coming, I am sure they would have made other preparations. That's why the neighborhood looks uncertain and seems like the day and night together.

The night in which many live gets darker and darker and threatens to cover all the hours; only if we take more of the light of Jesus to those forgotten places will the darkness continue to give ground. But the problem is: Who will take it?

Could this be a good ending for a book? Who said books should have an end?

Appendix

Places where Adulam is working as this book goes to press:

Comunidad Aljaba
Calle Soldado O. Sosa 1450 (Ex Rafaela)
Rafael Castillo – Partido de La Matanza – Pcia. de Buenos Aires

Adulam I
Calle Angélica 5835
Virrey del Pino – Partido de La Matanza – Pcia. de Buenos Aires

Adulam II – Pontevedra
Calle Monteagudo 2552
Pontevedra – Partido de Merlo – Pcia. de Buenos Aires

Adulam III – Hogar Miguel
Calle Deán Funes 2060
Pontevedra – Partido de Merlo – Pcia. de Buenos Aires

Adulam IV – Ciudad Deseada Km 33
Calle Villanueva 1184
González Catán – Partido de La Matanza – Pcia. de Buenos Aires

Hora feliz y Centro de día Sarah
Calle Bouchard 3035 – Barrio El Torero
Rafael Castillo – Partido de La Matanza – Pcia. de Buenos Aires

Hora Feliz y Comedor Soy de Jesús
Calle Finlay 1656 – Barrio San Cayetano
Rafael Castillo – Partido de La Matanza – Pcia. de Buenos Aires

Hora Feliz para niños Aprendiendo de Jesús
Barrio América
Rafael Castillo – Partido de La Matanza – Pcia. de Buenos Aires

Hora Feliz para niños Ríos de Agua Viva
Rafael Castillo – Partido de La Matanza – Pcia. de Buenos Aires

Hora Feliz y Comedor para niños Caminando con Jesús
Calle Soldado O. Sosa 1450 (Ex Rafaela)
Rafael Castillo – Partido de La Matanza – Pcia. de Buenos Aires

Hora Feliz y Centro de Reunión Villa Celina
Calle Caaguazú 2556
Villa Celina – Partido de La Matanza – Pcia. de Buenos Aires

Hora Feliz para niños Km 47
Barrio Sarmiento – Partido de La Matanza – Pcia. de Buenos Aires

Comunidad y Depósito
Calle Lope de Vega 1679
Rafael Castillo – Partido de La Matanza – Pcia. de Buenos Aires

Sede Social y centro de reunión
Calle Av. Libertad 1574 – Tres Arroyos – Pcia. de Buenos Aires

Hora Feliz para niños
Calle Neuquén s/n entre Antártida Argentina y Jujuy
Copetonas – Partido de Tres Arroyos – Pcia. de Buenos Aires

Granja del Peregrino
Camino de acceso a Copetonas y cruce a Oriente – Cuartel 9°
Zona Rural – Partido de Tres Arroyos – Pcia. de Buenos Aires

Centro de Ayuda Integral
Calle Belgrano 389
Oriente – Partido de Coronel Dorrego – Pcia. de Buenos Aires

Hora Feliz y Congregación Colonia El Saltito
Departamento 25 de Mayo – Pcia. de Misiones

Mission areas:

Misión Bilgai – Crusade of free toy giveaway for children.
Permanent support team to the Guaraníes in the province of Misiones.
Operación David – Adulam's hand outstretched to other ministries.
Misión Sinfonía – Permanent campaign of footwear for children.
Adulam Misionero – Missions and extension of the work
Adulam en Calle – Evangelism and help for children in the streets.
Teather – Compañía Adulam. Evangelism through art events.
Adulam Comunicaciones – Spreading of the message of Jesus through different media: Films, TV and Radio.
Editorial – Ediciones Adulam.
Main Office – Documents, finances, and administration
Literacy campaign for children and adults.
Misión "Amor" – Help for children with disabilities.
Help for the drug addict – Advising office and help groups for drug addicts.
Ministry of evangelism and consolation "Sara"
Prison Ministry – Support, biblical teaching and literacy campaign.
Capellanía hospitalaria – Visits and evangelism in hospitals.
Women Department
Advancing Men
Youth Department
Teenager Group
Active children group "Luz de mi vida".

Business ventures:

Carpentry. Ice-cream Factory. Iron workshop. Green house. Organic compound factory. Storage buildings and general recycling. Forklift workshop. School of mechanics. Bakeries. Leather handcrafts. Community clothes storage. Logistics department. Exchanging of services and goods circle: CISA. Grocery and clothes shop. Community Food Group.

All this is for serving God and the needy.

You will find more information at:
www.adulam.org.ar

If you so desire, you may write to:
omargaitan@sinectis.com.ar
gcadulam@hotmail.com

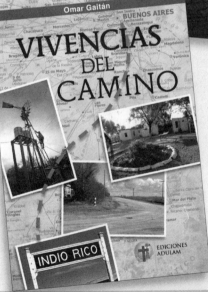